Elizabeth I
A Feminist Perspective

Elizabeth I

A Feminist Perspective

Susan Bassnett

Oxford • New York

First published in 1988 by
Berg Publishers
150 Cowley Road, Oxford, OX4 1JJ, UK
70 Washington Square South, New York, NY 10012, USA

Paperback edition reprinted in 1997

Berg is an imprint of Oxford International Publishers Ltd.

British Library Cataloguing in Publication Data
A catalogue record for this book is available from the British Library.

Library of Congress Cataloging-in-Publication Data
A catalogue record for this book is available from the Library of Congress.

ISBN 0 907582 98 2

Printed in Great Britain by WBC Book Manufacturers, Mid-Glamorgan.

To my Mother

Contents

Illustrations

(between pages 80 and 81)

1. Portrait of Elizabeth as a young girl. Artist unknown, c. 1542–7. Windsor Castle. Reproduced by kind permission of HM the Queen.

2. The Coronation Portrait. Artist unknown, c. 1559. Reproduced by kind permission of the Trustees of the National Portrait Gallery.

3. Chalk drawing of Elizabeth by Federigo Zuccaro, 1575. Reproduced by kind permission of the Trustees of the British Museum.

4. The Ditchley Portrait. Artist unknown, c. 1592. Reproduced by kind permission of the Trustees of the National Portrait Gallery.

5. Marble head of Elizabeth from her tomb in Westminster Abbey. Sculpted by Maximilian Colte and gilded by Nicholas Hilliard and John de Critz. Reproduced by kind permission of the Dean and Chapter of Westminster.

Genealogical table

Acknowledgements

I should like to thank Irene Pearson Renshaw, who typed the manuscript so beautifully. Thanks are also due, as always, to those people who make it possible for me to have the time in which to write at all: Yvonne Carpmail and Pat Corrie, the staff of the University of Warwick crèche, especially Anne Deas and Carol Miles, and my two eldest daughters Lucy and Vanessa.

SB

Introduction

In earth the first, in heaven the second Maid.

Elizabeth I is probably the most famous Englishwoman ever to have lived. She has been celebrated as a great stateswoman, during whose reign England acquired some degree of security in the troubled European arena and at the same time began to lay the foundations for its future empire. She presided over a country undergoing a cultural renaissance previously unimagined. By the time of her death at the age of seventy in 1603, she was being heralded as rival to the Virgin Mary, as a second Queen of Earth and Heaven, as a woman more than mortal women. Yet in the centuries since her death large numbers of historians, writers and musicians have been fascinated not so much by her divine attributes as by her earthly ones. She has provided subject-matter for innumerable books: seventy biographies have appeared since 1890 and it is impossible to list the enormous number of historical novels based on some part of her life. Her epic conflict with Mary Queen of Scots provided inspiration to Romantic writers from Schiller to Donizetti, who dramatised the struggle between what they perceived as two completely different female types, and made Elizabeth a familiar figure on the stage of both tragic and operatic theatre. In the twentieth century there have been film biographies *ad nauseam*, along with television biographies and plays, so that the image of a red-haired, white-faced woman in lavish gowns and a wide ruff has come to symbolise Elizabeth for millions of people who may never have actually read one of the many books about her.

What is still fascinating about Elizabeth is that all the writing and rewriting of her history, the multi-faceted depictions of a long-dead woman who reigned for forty-five years (a length of time that defeated all possible predictions when she first ascended the throne in 1558 after her sister Mary) nevertheless refuse to yield a coherent, consistent picture of her. We have portraits, some of her letters, some poems known to be hers and others attributed to her, some of her translations, and beyond that we

1

have a collection of intriguing and intensely biased eyewitness accounts of life close to her in at court. Even during her lifetime there were several Elizabeths, from the pure, chaste supporter of the Protestant cause who remedied the miseries wrought upon the English people during the reign of her bloody Catholic sister Mary to the diabolically motivated bastard daughter of Henry VIII whose lewd behaviour with her court favourites resulted in such portraits as the one described in a letter from Stafford to Walsingham in 1583, showing her on horseback 'with her right hande pullinge upp her clothes shewing her hindparte . . .'.[1] Between these two extreme views is a host of alternative perspectives, from which it is interesting to see how often assessments of Elizabeth are made by comparing her with Mary Queen of Scots. The crude line of argument presents Elizabeth as a shrewd, calculating, passionless figure, jealous of Mary's beauty and sensuous appeal. The apocryphal story about Elizabeth's reaction to the news of the birth of Mary's son, James, has it that she cried out: 'The Queen of Scots is delivered of a fair son, and I am but barren stock'.

The counter-argument depicts Mary as a silly, immature woman unable to handle the responsibilities of statecraft who lost both her throne and her head as a direct result of her incapacity for reasoned behaviour. This attitude is typified by G. B. Harrison, editor of Elizabeth's letters, who compares the handwriting of the two women, and ranks Elizabeth well above Mary: 'The Queen's handwriting in youth was beautiful, but in middle age it degenerated into a scrawl, very difficult to read, especially when she was writing French in a hurry, but a bold, resolute script nevertheless, running straight across the page, very different from the downhill schoolgirl hand of Mary Queen of Scots'.[2]

Years ago, when I supplemented the brief coverage of Tudor history taught in school with readings of historical novels (as my own daughter now does, a quarter of a century later), it became clear that the Elizabeth–Mary conflict so beloved of writers of literature and drama was to some extent still going on. Comic-book serials and historical novels plainly took sides; either you were for Mary or you were for Elizabeth. Long before I knew why, I supported Elizabeth's. It was not only that she seemed to be a winner, whereas Mary was the feminine victim incarnate, but because every account I read, in whatever form, gave me an image of a woman who was determined to live according to some private, inner pattern. She was, in short, a model of an independent woman for a girl growing up in the 1950s, long before the Women's Movement had announced itself. Although I was always in the minority, I still found myself standing up for Elizabeth.

Many of the novels (and indeed many of the supposedly more scholarly biographies) have shown a prurient fascination with Elizabeth's virginity. Sometimes writers simply refute it, citing the list of her supposed lovers, from Thomas Seymour in her teens, through the love of her life Robert Dudley, down to the Earl of Essex in her old age. The telling of these and other love stories varies considerably, but a predominating theme seems to be disappointment, starting with her first great passion for Seymour, executed in 1549 for treason when Elizabeth was sixteen, and ending with the quenching of her passion for Essex, whom she herself executed for the same offence in 1601. Elizabeth, the historical novelists repeatedly suggest, was unlucky in love; even her relationship with Dudley turned sour when he eventually married Lettice Knollys, former Countess of Essex and related to Elizabeth, whom Elizabeth detested. (This dislike of Lettice Knollys does not seem to be as fictional as some other assumptions; we can probably accept it, at least, as genuine.)

Other versions of Elizabeth's life struggle hard with the 'problem' of her virginity. Some biographers have stressed the 'masculinity' of her mind and, unwilling to deal with the issue of female sexuality, tend to brush over the question altogether. Others depict her as somehow maimed, damaged either by the Seymour affair or by an early memory of her mother's death. An extreme position is taken by Elizabeth Jenkins, in a biography that teeters on the edge of being a novel. She sees Elizabeth as sexually incomplete, a woman who was unable to have a satisfactory sex life because, in the dark corners of her memory, she equated sex with death. Her relationship with Dudley, according to Jenkins, stopped short of the sexual act, and although at one time Elizabeth had Dudley moved into a bedchamber next to her own, Jenkins believes that she never actually became his mistress. The following passage gives some idea of the heightened language many writers have used when dealing with this aspect of Elizabeth's life:

3

No one who saw her among men doubted her extreme suscepti-
bility to male attraction; it was in fact more than ordinary; but
it would seem that the harm done to Elizabeth as a small child
had resulted in an irremediable condition of nervous shock. . . .
Held up in the arms of her imploring mother to her terrible
father as he frowned down upon them; hearing that a sword
had cut off her mother's head: that her young stepmother had
been dragged shrieking down the gallery when she tried to
reach the King to entreat his mercy — these experiences, it
would appear, had built up a resistance that nothing, no
passion, no entreaty, no tenderness could conquer. In the
fatally vulnerable years she had learned to connect the idea of
sexual intercourse with terror and death; in the dark and
low-lying region of the mind where reason cannot penetrate she
knew that if you give yourself to men, they cut your head off
with a sword, an axe. The blood-stained key that frightens the
girl in 'Blue-Beard' is a symbol merely of the sexual act; in
Elizabeth's case, the symbol had a frightful actuality of its
own. It was the executioner's steel blade, running with blood.[3]

This kind of armchair psychoanalysis seems to have been a
favourite pastime of biographers of Elizabeth, particularly in the
1940s and 1950s (Jenkins's book appeared in 1958). An interesting feature of the many works on Elizabeth is that each age
refashions her image according to its own culture. Books on
Elizabeth have frequently glorified her symbolic position as head
of a nation enjoying a Golden Age, and it is significant that in the
latter part of the nineteenth century, when British imperialism
was at its height, the image of Good Queen Bess and the glorious
England of Shakespeare, Drake and Raleigh was very much to
the fore. Likewise, the work of Sir John Neale, whose biography
first appeared in 1934 and resulted in a whole crop of books in the
period following the Second World War, paints a picture of a
magnificent woman, Queen of a proud little nation fighting
against the threat of foreign invasion. The parallels between the
England that resisted the threat of Nazi Germany and the one
that withstood the might of Catholic Spain were forcibly made.
The Spanish Armada in 1588 and the Battle of Britain in 1940
were offered for comparison by historians, novelists and film-
makers of the 1940s and early 1950s.

The variations are endless: Elizabeth was glorious or diaboli-
cal; a magnificent stateswoman or an unfortunate neurotic case-

study; a hard masculine woman, or a gently feminine one unlucky in the choice of men in whom she placed her trust. All these characters derive from the ideological position of the writer who describes them. Most recently, yet another version of Elizabeth has appeared, a narrow feminist perspective that accuses her of not having done enough for other women, in much the same terms as Margaret Thatcher might be accused today, but with the difference, of course, that feminist ideology conceived in such terms did not exist in the sixteenth century.[4] Elizabeth would have perceived women as biologically different from men, as occupying different social roles, her notion of the relative positions of men and women in society would have been a Renaissance view, quite unlike that of the twentieth century.

The great division between Elizabeth and twentieth-century readers is time itself. In the four hundred years since her death, perceptions have changed so completely that we can only with great difficulty imagine how the Renaissance mind worked. Ideas about death provide an illuminating comparison. The particular horrors of public execution mean one thing today; they had quite another meaning in an age when death from plague, smallpox, leprosy and cholera was commonplace, when teeth rotted in one's head and open cancers crawled with maggots. Elizabeth's early life was indeed traumatic; but in adulthood she was certainly not squeamish about ordering bloodshed about her. Bear- and dog-baiting were among her favourite amusements and when the torture of suspects was required she did not hold back. To argue that she may have been maimed by imaginary visions of the headsman's axe is absurd; it is equally absurd to argue that Elizabeth could somehow have used her position to further the cause of women, in an age when such a concept would have been greeted with incomprehension.

In the preparation of this book I read and reread dozens of accounts of the life and times of Elizabeth, those purporting to be historical studies and those claiming to be works of fiction. As I read I kept waiting for a point of contact, for a channel of communication to be opened through which I could reach for Elizabeth across the gulf of time. It was perhaps predictable that there was no sudden breakthrough, no startling revelation. Instead, I found that while some of the more extravagant depictions of Elizabeth were easy to reject it was only after considering everything written about her that I began to formulate a reliable impression, and that impression is very close to the one I first had in my teens. It is an impression of a woman of energy and cunning, a woman of intelligence and feeling who was determined to survive. What some biographers have seen as Elizabeth's deviousness, I perceive as her skill in dodging and weaving and refusing to be pinned down. A splendid example of this facility may be found in the letters of the Count de Feria, ambassador in London of Philip II of Spain in the tense period immediately after Elizabeth's accession.

The widower of her sister Mary, Philip planned to begin negotiations to marry Elizabeth and secure his foothold in England. A few days after Mary's death in November 1558 de Feria wrote: 'although as I have written to your Majesty it is very early yet to talk about marriage, the confusion and ineptitude of these people in all their affairs make it necessary for us to be the more circumspect, so as not to miss the opportunities which are presented to us, and particularly in the matter of marriage'.[5]

Later in the same letter he added that the more he thought about the whole business, the more convinced he was becoming that 'everything depends upon the husband this woman marries'. Three weeks later, on 14 December, he wrote to the King that she was 'a very strange sort of woman', and early in 1559 in a long memorandum de Feria relates with some irritation the tactics Elizabeth was using to keep Philip's offer of marriage at arm's length. Firstly, Elizabeth discovered an impediment to the marriage in the fact of Philip having first married her sister Mary. This of course was a similar obstacle to the one her father, Henry VIII, claimed to have necessitated the dissolution of his marriage to Catherine of Aragon, thus enabling him to marry Elizabeth's mother Anne Boleyn. This argument had to be used with care, however, and de Feria writes that, having said this, Elizabeth seems to have considered the religious implications of what she was claiming and 'she denied point-blank the Pope's power which she had previously pointed out indirectly'. Next, she tried the argument that the people did not wish her to marry a foreigner. Finally: 'that several persons had told her that Your Majesty would come here and then go off to Spain directly. This she said with great laughter as if she could read the Count's secret thoughts. She is so well-informed about this that it looks as if she had seen His Majesty's letters. This should be taken good note of'.

De Feria's account of Elizabeth's strategies reveals several things about her. Firstly, that she was constantly on her guard and determined not to be caught out in argument; secondly, that she had taken the precaution of discovering as much as possible about the opposition, thirdly, that she had a strong sense of humour. That sense of humour comes up again, in a letter from de Feria of 11 April 1559, when he writes that she had mockingly suggested that King Philip could not have been so much in love with her as he had claimed to be, since he appeared unwilling to wait even four months for her. In fact, he gave up waiting and the question of marriage with Elizabeth was quietly dropped from the agenda.

Her sense of humour, which is testified to in all kinds of accounts, went hand-in-hand with great shrewdness. Elizabeth was astute enough to realise that Mary's government had suffered badly from her lack of skilled advisers, and she set about appointing men around her in whom she could place absolute trust. Although loose comparisons are made from time to time, between Elizabeth and Margaret Thatcher, the British Prime Minister in the age of Elizabeth II, they could not be further from the truth. Thatcher surrounds herself with weak men whom she is able to control and manipulate. The history of dismissals and resignations from her Cabinet is a story of the gradual loss of men who might have posed an intelligent and coherent alternative. Elizabeth, on the contrary, surrounded herself with strong men, and her relationship with the two Cecils, father and son, which lasted throughout her reign, is a classic example of this process in action. Moreover, in setting up her Council, Elizabeth also chose men determined, as she was, on survival; the establishment of the complex spy networks and policing systems that characterised her reign shows the extent to which those in power were determined to hold on to their positions. Even so, having set up her advisory group, Elizabeth did not put ultimate control into their hands. Her strongest weapon seems to have been one that none of them could fight against successfully — her unpredictability. When driven into a corner Elizabeth would procrastinate, change her mind, tear up documents she had signed, keep petitioners waiting for an indefinite period and use any means at her disposal to break down their confidence. De Feria notes that one of her first moves on being hailed as Queen was to make a speech to her women ordering them never to speak to her on business matters, and although this system was occasionally breached, she tried hard to keep a space round herself in which she could not be harried. The signing of the death warrant for Mary Queen of Scots was one of the rare occasions when Elizabeth's advisers prevailed over her. That she felt cheated by them is shown by her manifest anger: she sent her Secretary Davison to the Tower, and wrote a somewhat distressed letter to James VI, Mary's son:

> My dear Brother, I would you knew (though not felt) the extreme dolor that overwhelms my mind, for that miserable accident which (far contrary to my meaning) hath befallen. . . . I am not so base-minded that fear of any living creature or Prince should make me afraid to do that were just; or done, to deny the same. I am not of so base a lineage, nor carry so vile a mind. But, as not to disguise, fits not a King, so will I never dissemble my actions, but cause them show even as I meant them. Thus assuring yourself of me, that as I know this was deserved, yet if I had meant it I would never lay it on others' shoulders; no more will I not damnify myself that thought it not.[6]

It is not therefore to be wondered at that Burghley (William Cecil was ennobled by Elizabeth in 1571 and took the title Lord Burghley) complained that '[the] lack of a resolute answer from her Majesty driveth to the wall'.[7]

There are countless stories of Elizabeth's abrupt changes of heart, which have sometimes been perceived as an example of feminine capriciousness. In 1560, for example, after yielding to persuasion by Robert Dudley to make him earl, she changed her mind after the patent had been drawn up and cut it into pieces with a knife. Equally famous is the lengthy saga of Elizabeth's proposed marriage to the Duke of Alençon, which reached its greatest absurdity in 1581 when, as Mendoza, the Spanish ambassador relates, Elizabeth publicly kissed Alençon on the mouth, gave him a ring from her own hand as a token and announced that he would be her husband. Less than a month later she was busy negotiating a sum of money that would be sufficient to persuade Alençon to go to the Low Countries to fight

8

the Spanish, well out of reach of any possible marriage bargaining. Her life story is full of examples of this kind of behaviour, of grand gestures designed to deceive the onlooker into believing the opposite of Elizabeth's real intentions, or simply part of a deliberate plan not to reveal precisely what she was thinking.

It would be patronising and unjust to continue to dismiss such behaviour simply as evidence of one woman's instability. A close look at the early years of Elizabeth's life shows that she needed to keep people guessing, as she steered her careful path through the religious, political and emotional minefield that surrounded her. When in 1549 at the age of sixteen she was questioned by Sir Robert Tyrwhit to discover the precise nature of her relationship with Thomas Seymour, who had been arrested on a charge of plotting to ovethrow the throne, Tyrwhit was forced to admit that 'she hath a very good wit and nothing is gotten of her but by great policy'.[8] During that same interrogation, Tyrwhit also noted Elizabeth's loyalty to her two servants, Catherine Ashley and Thomas Parry, who remained with her until their respective deaths in 1565 and 1560: 'in no way will she confess any practice by Mistress Ashley or the cofferer [Parry] concerning my Lord Admiral [Seymour]; and yet I do see it in her face that she is guilty and do perceive as yet she will abide more storms ere she accuse Mistress Ashley'.

The depiction of Elizabeth as whimsical and capricious is belied by the intense loyalty she showed to her friends and servants throughout her life. When Cecil was dying he wrote to his son, Robert, that Elizabeth fed him daily with a spoon, and she took a great interest in the health of those close to her, often sending them patent remedies and nourishing broths. Among her letters, two in particular show her concern for the afflictions of her friends. A letter to Lady Catherine Knollys, wife of Sir Francis Knollys and first cousin to Elizabeth, written in 1553, assures the recipient of Elizabeth's constant loyalty and friendship, despite the fact that the couple had fled overseas into exile to escape persecution by Queen Mary. It is a simple letter, but full of feeling: 'The length of time, and distance of place, separates not the love of friends, nor deprives not the show of good will. . . . My power but small, my love as great as them whose gifts may tell their friendship's tale, let will supply all other want and often sending take the lieu of often sights'.[9] The letter is signed by 'your loving cousin and ready friend, COR ROTTO [Broken Heart]'.

Much later, towards the end of her life, there is a letter written in her own handwriting to Lady Norris, after hearing that Lady Norris's son had died in the wars in Ireland. Elizabeth addresses Lady Norris as 'Mine own Crow' (she gave nicknames to many of those close to her — Dudley was her 'Eyes', Sir Christopher Hatton her 'Mutton', Cecil 'Sir Spirit') and writes in a style that shows her own distress:

> We resolved no longer to smother either our care for your sorrow, or the sympathy of our grief for his love, wherein, if it be true that society in sorrow works diminution, we do assure you, by this true messenger of our mind, that nature can have stirred no more dolorous affection in you as a mother for a dear son, than gratefulness and memory of his services past hath wrought in us, his sovereign, apprehension of our miss of so worthy a servant.[10]

Nevertheless, though she could be loyal to friends and capable of deep feelings, she could also be spiteful and vindictive. Carolly Erikson's biography, published in 1983, offers a glimpse of some of the negative aspects of Elizabeth's character — the beating of her maids, the slapping of people who disagreed with her, the imprisonment of the court ladies who dared to marry without her consent, — or worse, to become pregnant, — and the vanity that resulted in a need for flattery and sycophancy which her reason must have told her was nonsensical. Erikson suggests that much of this behaviour resulted from her spinsterhood, from her failure to have children and her consequent envy of those women who did manage to have husbands and children. Erikson sums up the options open to Elizabeth in the following terms:

> From the start, it had never really been a fair choice. Either she had to go the way of her tragic half-sister Mary, who by taking a husband had traded what precarious authority she possessed for the privation and humiliation of a loveless royal marriage, ending as a victim of the enmity and feigned fidelity that sorrounded her. Or she had to endure the extreme ultimately dangerous approval of the men in government — not to mention the shame of public scorn and the undercurrent of ridicule and ugly gossip at court and elsewhere — by remaining single.

The second course had seemed the wiser one, and the one best suited to Elizabeth's temperament and gifts. Yet spinsterhood hobbled and wounded her; she cannot have relished her eccentricities, or the foul reputation that followed her, or the poisonous atmosphere of her bedchamber, even though she relished the very real sovereignty she wielded in their despite.[11]

Certainly if she had had twentieth-century sensibilities she would have found such a lifestyle unbearable; but if we take an imaginative leap backwards into the Elizabethan age it is easier to come to terms with some of the apparent contradictions in Elizabeth's life. I find it hard to accept that a decision *not* to have children and *not* to marry necessarily affects a woman negatively, and in Elizabeth's case, living at a time when for the majority of nobly born women marriage was certainly not made in heaven, her choice was prudent and not so unusual as some biographers have made out. There is no doubt that in the early years of her reign the succession question was the cause of considerable disquiet and led to much of the pressure on her to marry, but once James Stuart had been designated as a suitable successor, the pressure diminished. What is also often forgotten is that Elizabeth lived in a world where formal behaviour played a very important role, and the elaborate sequence of flattery and obsequies that surrounded her must be seen in terms of ritual rather than in terms of realistic demonstrations of feeling.

Some indication of the rituals by which she lived is given in eyewitness accounts of life at court. The German lawyer Paul Hentzner kept a journal of his travels in England in 1598 and provides an account of a state reception at Greenwich, at which Elizabeth appeared dressed in white silk, with long train and a crown on her head: 'wherever she turned her face as she was going along, everybody fell down on their knees'. Hentzner then records the ceremonial serving of Elizabeth's dinner:

A gentleman entered the room bearing a rod, and along with him another who had a table-cloth, which after they had both knelt three times, with the utmost veneration, he spread upon the table, and after kneeling again, they both retired. Then came two others, one with the rod again, the other with a salt-cellar, a plate and bread; when they had knelt as the others had done, and placed what was brought upon the table, they

11

too retired with the same ceremonies performed by the first. At last came an unmarried lady of extraordinary beauty (we were told that she was a countess) and along with her a married one, bearing a tasting-knife; the former was dressed in white silk, who, when she had prostrated herself three times, in the most graceful manner approached the table and rubbed the plates with bread and salt with as much awe as if the Queen had been present. When they had waited there a little while, the yeomen of the guard entered, bareheaded, clothed in scarlet, with a golden rose upon their backs, bringing in at each turn a course of twenty four dishes, served in silver most of it gilt; these dishes were received by a gentleman in the same order as they were brought and placed upon the table, while the lady-taster gave to each of the guard a mouthful to eat of the particular dish he had brought, for fear of any poison. During the time that this guard, which consists of the tallest and stoutest men that can be found in all England, 100 in number, being carefully selected for this service, were bringing dinner, twelve trumpets and two kettle-drums made the hall ring for half-an-hour together. At the end of this ceremonial, a number of unmarried ladies appeared, who with particular solemnity lifted the meat off the table, and conveyed it into the Queen's inner and more private chamber, where after she had chosen for herself, the rest goes to the ladies of the court. The Queen dines and sups alone with very few attendants; and it is very seldom that any body, foreigner or native, is admitted at that time, and then only at the intercession of some distinguished personage.[12]

This account gives some idea of the life Elizabeth led; surrounded by elaborate ceremony, nevertheless she chose to eat alone in her room. Behind the complex ritual of quasi-religious magnificence lay the simple but crucial task of checking food for poison. Elizabeth lived in a world where violent death could come in many forms, from poisoned food or gloves, from a knife in the back, a shot or, ultimately, through deposition and the headsman's axe. Each time she heard of the death of members of the European ruling houses by some form of treachery or by armed revolt she must have become yet more uncertain about her own security. The rituals served a purpose; they served to ensure that nothing unexpected or untoward happened unnoticed in the bustle of court life. It is important to remember that security was difficult to maintain, since Elizabeth's court, like that of any Renaissance ruler, kept constantly moving from palace to palace to enable the potentially lethal cesspits to be cleaned regularly. These rituals also served to remind the courtiers who thronged about the Queen, many of whom had ambiguous feelings about her claim to the throne, that she alone was supreme ruler. She herself, however, preferred to dine in the privacy of her own room, away from the public gaze that followed her at all other times.

Accounts of Elizabeth's eating habits show that she ate sparingly, an unusual practice in an age when many courtiers ate and drank to excess. Throughout her life she seems to have taken great care of her body, exercising regularly and eating lightly, and she continued to hunt, dance and take long daily walks until the last months of her life. These practices accord with the picture of a woman who wanted to stay in control, who sought not so much to prolong her life but rather to remain in full possession of all her physical and mental faculties for as long as possible. Behind this careful lifestyle lay the fear not only of death by treacherous means but also of ill-health. In her youth, Elizabeth is recorded as suffering from fairly frequent colds, influenzas and nameless illnesses, and although some of these may have been tactical (when summoned to London from Ashbridge by Mary in January 1554 Elizabeth pleaded illness and refused to move, for fear that she might be arrested and sent to the Tower if she obeyed Mary's command), others may have been stress-induced. For such a tough woman, she was also very afraid of allowing others to perform surgery on her body or to treat her. She suffered badly from toothache throughout her life, and one of the first pieces of information we have about her is a report from her governess, Lady Bryan, saying that 'my Lady hath great pain with her great teeth, and they come very slowly forth . . . .'.[13] Eyewitnesses describe her teeth in old age as 'black' and in one extraordinary episode in 1578 she was so terrified of having a rotten tooth pulled that Bishop Aylmer volunteered to have a tooth removed in her presence, to prove to her that the pain could be borne. In 1562 she contracted smallpox and came close to death. She recovered, relatively unmarked by the disease, though Robert Dudley's sister, Mary Sidney, who nursed her devotedly throughout the illness, also caught smallpox and was badly disfigured.

13

Accounts of Elizabeth's physical appearance vary as much as accounts of her personality. We do know that later in life she wore a wig, but so also did many courtiers, both male and female, and the image that has sometimes been presented of a ludicrous old hag, her face covered in white-lead paint, wearing an orange curled wig and emulating youthful beauty is probably unfair, in that Elizabeth would have been surrounded with painted, be-wigged and over-dressed court attendants of all ages and would not have been unusual. She does seem to have refused to adapt her appearance to old age, however, and continued to insist on public signs of virginity, such as wearing her hair loose, along with public gestures of flamboyant majesty, dying the tails and manes of her horses orange to match the wigs she had placed over her natural grey hair.

Portraits of Elizabeth abound, but according to Roy Strong, probably only the portrait by Federigo Zuccaro (c. 1574–5) (see plate 3) and the image on her tomb (plate 5) can be 'established on a documentary basis as being a direct record of her features'.[14] Sir John Hayward, who wrote his account of Elizabeth just a few years after her death, left a physical description of her upon which biographers and novelists have drawn ever since:

> Shee was a Lady, upon whom nature had bestowed, and well-placed, many of her fayrest favours; of stature meane, slender, streight, and amiably composed; of such state in her carriage, as every motione of her seemed to beare majesty: her haire was inclined to pale yellow, her foreheade large and faire, a seemeing sete for princely grace; her eyes lively and sweete, but short-sighted; her nose somewhat rising in the middest; the whole compasse of her countenance somewhat long, but yet of admirable beauty, not so much in that which is tearmed the flower of youth, as in a most delightfull compositione of majesty and modesty in equall mixture.[15]

Not beautiful, but striking, giving the impression of being tall, even though accounts vary, with some claiming she was short, others that she was taller than average. What everyone seems to have agreed upon is that she prided herself on having beautiful hands, which she showed off at all opportunities and which are frequently in the foreground of her portraits. She also prided herself on her fair complexion, wearing low-cut dresses well into

14

old age. From the Tudors she inherited her reddish hair and short-sightedness, and it is tempting to follow the path trodden by many historical novelists and suggest that from her mother, Anne Boleyn, she inherited a personal charisma that made her seem beautiful even though she lacked many of the attributes necessary to be declared beautiful in Renaissance terms. Certainly throughout her reign, her dynamic energy impressed itself on people she encountered. She was primarily a woman of movement, a woman who could not sit still for long. When she did finally sit still, collapsing on to cushions on the floor and refusing to move for days, it was a clear sign that she was about to die.

Elizabeth died unmajestically. She gradually disintegrated in body and mind, after lying on her cushions and refusing food for ten days. On 21 March 1603 she was finally persuaded to change her clothes and got to bed, but she died three days later, on 24 March, sinking into silence and immobility, all the energy spent. Yet, as Sir John Neale records, on 6 February, just weeks before that final collapse, she had presided over an audience with the Venetian envoy, wearing elaborate ceremonial dress, with an imperial crown on her head, and had reproved the envoy because Venice had not sent a resident ambassador to England, pointing out that she should not be treated differently from other princes simply because she was a woman, 'for my sex cannot diminish my prestige'.[16] That much is certain from all the many and various versions of Elizabeth's life and work — not only did her sex never diminish her prestige, it actually enhanced it. And that, in an age when the social value of women was in retreat, is a unique and extraordinary achievement.

Notes

1. Letter from Stafford to Walsingham, 17 November 1583, quoted in Roy Strong, *Portraits of Queen Elizabeth I* (Oxford: Clarendon Press, 1963), p. 32.
2. G. B. Harrison, *The Letters of Queen Elizabeth* (London: Cassell, 1935), p. xiv.

3. Elizabeth Jenkins, *Elizabeth the Great* (Watford: Odhams, 1958), pp. 95–6.
4. As an example of this approach, see Alison Heisch, 'Queen Elizabeth I and the persistence of Patriarchy', *Feminist Review*, no. 4 (1980), pp. 45–75.
5. Letter from Count de Feria to King Philip, 21 November 1558, *Calendar of State Papers, Spanish, Elizabethan*, 4 vols., ed. M. A. S. Hume (London: Her Majesty's Stationery Office, 1892–9).
6. Letter from Elizabeth to James I, 14 February 1587, repr. in Harrison, *Letters*, p. 188.
7. Conyers Read, *Lord Burghley and Queen Elizabeth* (London: Cape, 1960), p. 528.
8. *A Collection of State Papers Relating to Affairs in the Reigns of King Henry VIII, King Edward VI, Queen Mary, and Queen Elizabeth . . . left by William Cecil, Lord Burghley, and now remaining at Hatfield House*, 2 vols., Samuel Haynes and William Murdin (London: 1740, 1757), vol. 0, p. 69.
9. Letter from Elizabeth to Lady Catherine Knollys, 1553, repr. in Harrison, *Letters*, p. 19.
10. Letter from Elizabeth to Lady Norris, 22 September 1597, repr. ibid., p. 250.
11. Carolly Erikson, *The First Elizabeth* (London: Macmillan, 1983), pp. 264–5.
12. Extracts from Paul Hentzner's Travels in England, 1598, in William Brenckley Rye (ed.), *England as Seen by Foreigners in the days of Elizabeth and James the First* (London: John Russell Smith, 1865), pp. 105–7.
13. Letter from Lady Bryan to Lord Cromwell, 1536, repr. in Frank A. Mumby, *The Girlhood of Queen Elizabeth: A Narrative in Contemporary Letters* (London: Constable, 1909), pp. 16–18.
14. Strong, *Portraits*, p. 17.
15. John Hayward, *Annals of the First Four Years of the Reign of Queen Elizabeth*, ed. John Bruce, Camden Society, Old Series, VII (London: J. B. Nichols, 1840).
16. J. E. Neale, *Queen Elizabeth I* (London: Cape, 1934; repr. Harmondsworth: Penguin, 1952), p. 395 (Penguin edn.).

1 Bastard and Princess

Elizabeth was born on Sunday, 7 September 1533, between 3 and 4 in the afternoon at the palace of Greenwich. Her astrological sign was Virgo, the Virgin, appropriate enough for the woman who was to remain unmarried throughout her life and be celebrated as Gloriana, Cynthia, Astraea, Diana and Faerie Queen, and of whom Giordano Bruno, the great Renaissance philosopher, spoke in the following terms:

> Of Elizabeth I speak, who by her title and royal dignity is inferior to no other monarch in the world; who for her wisdom and skill in sound government is second to none of those who hold the sceptre. I leave it to the world to judge what place she takes among all other princes for her knowledge of arts and sciences and for her fluency in all the tongues. . If her earthly territory were a true reflection of the width and grandeur of her spirit this great Amphitrite would bring far horizons within her girdle and enlarge the circumference of her dominion to include not only Britain and Ireland but some new world, as vast as the universal frame, where her all-powerful hand should have full scope to raise a united monarchy.[1]

When Elizabeth first entered the world it would have seemed inconceivable that she might one day have received such lavish praise. For the most striking feature of Elizabeth's birth is that she was of the wrong sex. Her father, Henry VIII had married her mother, Anne Boleyn, early in 1533 when she had become pregnant; he had finally divorced his former wife, Catherine of Aragon, a few months earlier. The long and bitter divorce battle had disturbed both the peace of the realm and Henry's own state of mind. Along with his physical passion for Anne Boleyn was the earnest desire for a male heir; his sole surviving child from his first marriage was the seventeen-year-old Mary, a devout Catholic who had suffered intensely from her father's rejection of her mother and subsequent movement away from the authority of the Pope. Catherine's Spanish ancestry had meant that pressure could be brought to bear on the Pope to oppose Henry's divorce proceedings, and the rift between Rome and the English Church was never to be healed.

The prince expected by Anne Boleyn was therefore of huge symbolic significance. He was to be heir to the throne of England and the first child born to a monarch who took upon himself the claim to be head of the Church. The child would therefore be a true child of the English Reformation, the herald of a new era. When it was born and turned out to be female the news caused consternation. Writing to his master, the Emperor Charles V, Eustace Chapuys noted that:

> On Sunday last, on the eve of Lady Day, about 3 o'clock in the afternoon, the King's mistress was delivered of a girl, to the great disappointment and sorrow of the King, of the Lady herself, and of others of her party, and to the great shame and confusion of physicians, astrologers, wizards, and witches, all of whom affirmed that it would be a boy.[2]

Henry at first seems to have intended to christen the baby Mary, so that the first Mary, Catherine of Aragon's daughter, would be truly supplanted, in name as well as in title and inheritance, but when the christening took place on 10 September, the new child was given the name Elizabeth. Moreover, while Elizabeth was given the title of Princess, Mary was demoted to the title Lady Mary and declared illegitimate. Princess Elizabeth was installed with a large household at Hatfield, while Mary's retinue was cut down and she was ordered to serve her new baby sister as lady-in-waiting. All that Mary could do was to fight a guerrilla war over small details of precedence and protocol, and whatever the later, adult relationship between the two sisters, it is difficult to imagine that it could have begun with anything but deep hostility on Mary's part towards the new baby who had, simply by being born, deprived her of her parents, her status and her prospects for the future.

By the time Elizabeth was two, relations between Henry and Anne had deteriorated past any redemption. Henry was already paying court to Jane Seymour, the woman who became his third wife and finally gave him the son he longed for, the sickly, ill-fated Edward VI, when Anne miscarried of a male child. In May 1536 Anne was beheaded on Tower Green on charges of adultery, and ten days later Henry married again. Elizabeth, who had enjoyed barely two-and-a-half years of preferential treatment, was declared a bastard and relegated to the same status as Mary. As had also happened to Mary, this demotion meant an immediate change in financial status. A letter from Lady Bryan, Elizabeth's governess, to Lord Cromwell, the Protector and controller of the purse strings, paints a gloomy portrait of the baby princess's poverty: 'she hath neither gown, nor kirtle, nor petticoat, nor no manner of linen nor smocks, nor kerchiefs, nor rails [night dresses], nor body stitchets [corsets], nor handkerchiefs, nor sleeves, nor mufflers, nor biggens [night-caps]'.[3]

Towards the end of 1536 Lady Bryan's place was taken by Catherine Champernowne, who later married John Ashley, a gentleman of Elizabeth's household, and as Catherine or 'Kat' Ashley became perhaps the closest to a mother-figure that Elizabeth ever knew. Blanche and Thomas Parry also joined Elizabeth's household at the same time, and all three were to remain as loyal to Elizabeth as she was to them, playing a significant part in the troubled years of Elizabeth's early life.

There has been considerable speculation about the impact on Elizabeth of her mother's death. One immediate result was that in addition to Henry declaring her to be illegitimate, gossip suggested that her father might not have been the King at all, but one of the men with whom Anne Boleyn had been accused of adultery. This particular slander lurked in the shadows throughout Elizabeth's life; Mary, her sister, repeated it shortly before she died and for generations it provided fuel for anti-Elizabeth propagandists. Once she became Queen, however, Elizabeth seems to have risen above jibes of this kind, though it is an interesting detail in her life that she made very few public gestures towards the rehabilitation of her mother. Paul Johnson, in his splendidly detailed study of Elizabeth, compares this lack of public recognition to Mary's elaborate gestures on behalf of her own mother after she came to power. His explanation for this behaviour of Elizabeth is very perceptive:

Elizabeth was a practical woman: she had no wish to reopen old sores and re-fight the battles of the past purely to satisfy her personal feelings of self-esteem. It is the first evidence we possess of her almost total lack of dynastic enthusiasm, so very uncharacteristic of her age. But, being a practical woman, she was generous, within limits, to her Boleyn relations.[4]

Johnson interprets Elizabeth's behaviour as being pragmatic and practical, in line with her tendency to mediate rather than meet in head-on conflict forces that might have threatened or opposed her. What he describes as her 'lack of dynastic enthusiasm' showed itself in two ways: on the one hand she made few statements extolling her ancestry, and on the other she refused to marry and bear an heir herself, thereby allowing the Tudor line to die out altogether and be replaced by their distant cousins the Stuarts.

Jane Seymour died in 1537 when Elizabeth was four years old. Henry was married three times more; to Anne of Cleves, from whom he separated almost immediately in 1540; to Catherine Howard, cousin of Anne Boleyn, who also died on the block in 1542; and finally, to Catherine Parr who outlived him and to whom Elizabeth wrote in 1544 when Henry had gone to France and Catherine had been appointed General Regent of the Realm in his absence. This is the first surviving letter written by Elizabeth; it is in Italian and uses the image she clearly favoured, that of envious Fortune whose revolving wheel brings her discontent as well as happiness. There have been claims for other earlier letters, and Agnes Strickland's study of Elizabeth in her *Lives of the Queens of England* (1851) quotes a letter supposedly from Elizabeth to Anne of Cleves, dated 1540. However, Agnes Strickland drew heavily on a seventeenth-century work by an Italian Gregorio Leti whose biography contained a number of letters that have been shown to be forgeries. Leti's fictitious letters of Elizabeth include some apparently written to Thomas Seymour, along with those sent from him in return, and correspondence between Elizabeth and Edward Courtenay, all of which purport to show that she was romantically involved with both men. Though the style of these letters, when contrasted with Elizabeth's other writing, is a strong clue to their unreliability, Leti's version of Elizabeth's life and his invented correspondence have been widely used by novelists and biographers alike. His version of her life clearly has great appeal to those who see it in a romantic light, who want to discover in Elizabeth's early years all kinds of deep emotional traumas and unfulfilled passions. Moreover, Leti's letters include exactly what sensationalist biographers would hope to find — protestations of love, rejections of marriage offers and frustrated hopes, which is no doubt why they have been so much quoted despite their falsity. Indeed the letters are worth reading, if only to understand the fascination that Elizabeth exerted over later generations of writers who have stretched their imaginations to the limit in attempts to understand her complex personality. I find it impossible, however, to take seriously a claim that Elizabeth might have written such a sentence as: 'Do me the justice to believe that my love for you is greater than yours can possibly be for me, and that I long to see you, so that you may hear from my own lips that which prudence forbids me to write'.[5] This is very much the tone and content of the novelette, and is completely at variance with the carefully controlled writing of those early letters whose authenticity is not in doubt.

The young Elizabeth was certainly not educated in the manner of a romantic heroine. When she was eleven years old, she sent as a gift to Catherine Parr her own translation of a work by Marguerite of Navarre, *The Glasse of the Synnefull Soule*, in a cover she had embroidered with blue and silver threads with clusters of purple flowers. The gift displayed three skills in one object — Elizabeth's ability to translate into elaborate literary English, her handwriting, and her needlework. She made several other similar books, one of which was dedicated to her father. This combination of practical and intellectual skills shows that Elizabeth's education followed the pattern of Humanist education for women established a generation earlier in her father's time. Catherine of Aragon had been taught by a woman, Beatrix Galindo, who was professor of rhetoric at the University of Salamanca, and her choice of tutors for her daughter Mary shows how highly she valued the notion of a wide-ranging curriculum. In 1523 she invited Juan Luis Vives to be director of Mary's studies, and Vives wrote two Latin treatises on the education of women, the best-known of which was translated by Richard Hyrde and printed in 1540 as *The Instruction of a Christian Woman*. Hyrde later wrote the introduction to a translation of a work by Erasmus by another learned woman Margaret Roper, daughter of Sir Thomas More, in which he set out some parameters for the further education of women. While both theoreticians extolled the virtues

21

of obedience for daughters and wives, and suggested that all women should be trained in housewifely and medicinal skills, both also proposed that learning would make women more attractive and help them to become ideal companions. The notion that a woman should be considered as companion rather than social and intellectual inferior was a radical departure from earlier views on the marriage relationship and the need for women's education.

In his study of learned ladies of the sixteenth and seventeenth centuries George Ballard gives the names of a large number of Elizabeth's contemporaries who were educated to a high degree.[6] From studies such as this, we have some idea of the way in which Humanist ideas of education affected both the role and the status of women, and it seems fair to say that although Elizabeth appears to have been an accomplished linguist, who prided herself on her ability to extemporise in Latin, French or Italian, this was by no means unusual. There has not yet been a detailed study of Elizabeth's female friends throughout her life, but what emerges from a survey of the evidence available is that she enjoyed the company of highly intelligent, cultured women. Among them were Mildred Coke, who married William Cecil, Lady Mary Sidney, mother of Philip Sidney, and Lady Norris, the friend she called her 'Black Crow'. Much has been made of Elizabeth's liking for the company of men and her jealousy of women she judged to be more sexually attractive than herself, but she was also an intellectual, a woman of cultivated tastes with a trained mind, and she seems to have held on to this serious side of her personality despite the frivolities and extravagant hypocrisy of court life.

In 1550 her tutor, Roger Ascham, writing to John Sturmius, paints a picture of a serious-minded, highly gifted sixteen year old. He comments on the number of ladies of his day whose learning is remarkable, adding that Elizabeth outshines them all. He praises her Latin and Greek, and his account of her taste and physical appearance is strongly reminiscent of the early portrait of Elizabeth painted some time in the 1540s (see plate 1):

The Lady Elizabeth has accomplished her sixteenth year; and so much solidity of understanding, such courtesy united with dignity, have never been observed at so early an age. She has the most ardent love of true religion and of the best kind of literature. The constitution of her mind is exempt from female weakness, and she is endued within a masculine power of application. No apprehension can be quicker than hers, no memory more retentive. French and Italian she speaks like English; Latin, with fluency, propriety and judgement; she also spoke Greek with me, frequently, willingly, and moderately well. Nothing can be more elegant than her handwriting, whether in the Greek or Roman character. In music she is very skilful, but does not greatly delight. With respect to personal decoration, she greatly prefers a simple elegance to show and splendour, so despising the 'outward adorning of plaiting the hair and of wearing of gold', that in the whole manner of her life she rather resembles Hippolyta than Phaedra.[7]

There are some curious features of Ascham's portrayal of Elizabeth. He singles out her linguistic ability and her magnificent handwriting, both of which were frequently admired throughout her life, but he suggests that she was not particularly fond of music and avoided elaborate clothes and jewellery. There are a number of testimonies which prove, in fact, exactly the opposite; Elizabeth was extremely fond of music and the lavishness of her clothes and jewels was constantly remarked upon by eyewitnesses. In her portraits we can trace a growing fascination for more and more ornament, and as she grew older so the size of her skirts grew larger, her ruffs deeper, her jewellery heavier and more obtrusive. She played the lute, lyre and virginals and was passionately devoted to dancing, while the music composed for her chapel royal was her special pride and delight. The image of a woman who preferred books to song and sober garments to jewel-encrusted gowns is at variance with the image of Elizabeth as Queen, and there were very particular reasons for this. The Elizabeth depicted by Roger Ascham was carefully creating an image of herself as a respectable, studious woman who despised frivolity — part of a calculated attempt to redeem her reputation which had been damaged by allegations of her illicit relationship with Thomas Seymour, her stepmother's husband.

The Seymour episode has fired the imagination of novelists for centuries, and it remains a disturbing and unsolved passage in Elizabeth's early life. Elizabeth was living with Catherine Parr at Chelsea in the period immediately following Henry VIII's death in 1547 and, although only fourteen years old, she was already considered to be of marriageable age. Proposals had been made for her hand, one of which had come from the flamboyant, aggressive Thomas Seymour, then aged thirty-eight, brother of the Edward Seymour who had been appointed Lord Protector for the young King Edward VI, who was still only nine years old. When the Royal Council declined Seymour's proposal he apparently began to court Catherine Parr, with whom he had formed an attachment before her marriage to the old King, and married her in secret. After the marriage Seymour moved into Catherine Parr's house and in the ensuing months, until Elizabeth left in the late spring of 1548, a relationship seems to have developed between Seymour and Elizabeth that caused serious doubts to be raised about Elizabeth's chastity.

Briefly, the allegations involved over-familiarity on Seymour's part, with horseplay in bed in the mornings, and Seymour habitually going into Elizabeth's bedroom half-dressed and striking her 'upon the buttocks familiarly'. One bizarre episode appears to have involved Catherine also, when Catherine held Elizabeth while Seymour 'cut her gown, being black cloth, into a hundred pieces'.[8] Certainly Kat Ashley was concerned about the propriety of Seymour's behaviour; gossip spread that he was having an affair with Elizabeth, that he planned to marry her after his wife, some twenty years older than Elizabeth, was dead or set aside, and even that Elizabeth was pregnant by him. Catherine Parr's role during these months is also dubious; she was pregnant for the first time at thirty-five, in those days a dangerous age to begin child-bearing, and all the evidence points to her having been deeply in love with Seymour. It may well be that she did as many other women have done who, because of the strength of their emotions, seem able to ignore a situation in the household involving infidelity or incest, which the exercise of reason would compel them to acknowledge. The fear engendered by a late pregnancy and the presence in the household of an energetic, attractive and intelligent younger woman who had already been sought after as a wife by her own husband cannot have been comfortable for her. In May 1548 Elizabeth left Chelsea; again, much has been made of this by biographers, many of whom have seen it as a sign of a crisis in the relationship between Elizabeth and Catherine. Catherine appears to have

24

believed that Elizabeth was emotionally involved with Seymour, and claimed to have seen her in the arms of a man, possibly Seymour, though this is not specified. The evidence of what took place in the months of this *ménage à trois* comes from the depositions made in 1549 by Elizabeth herself, Kat Ashley and Thomas Parry during the proceedings against Seymour after he had been accused of treason. This means that not only were all the statements made some time after the events had supposedly taken place, but they were made in very particular circumstances. Extracted under cross-examination, there are some differences in the versions, but the basic story is roughly similar and points to what can be described as sexual harassment of Elizabeth by Seymour, and extreme naïvety on Elizabeth's part that many have chosen to construe as evidence of her love for Seymour. Elizabeth certainly seems to have left Catherine Parr's household under a cloud, and she suffered an attack of one of her nervous diseases (migraine, sickness and eye-trouble) immediately afterwards, a sign of the stress she was under. In June 1548 she wrote a letter of thanks to her step-mother, signing herself 'Your Highness' humble daughter'. The letter is ambiguous and hints at difficulties between the two of them; Elizabeth expresses her anxiety at seeing Catherine 'undoubtful of health' and one complex sentence suggests that they may not have parted on the best of terms: 'if your Grace had not a good opinion of me, you would not have offered friendship to me that way at all, meaning the contrary'. A letter written to Thomas Seymour a month later is brief and tense: 'I am a friend not won with trifles, nor lost with the like', she writes, and signs herself: 'Your assured friend to my little power' — the phrase that she used time and again in her letters written before she acquired the safety of a throne.[9]

On 5 September 1548, just two days before Elizabeth's fifteenth birthday, Catherine Parr died of puerperal fever after giving birth to a daughter. Lady Jane Grey, Seymour's niece, was chief mourner, having taken Elizabeth's place in Catherine's household. Seymour now saw various opportunities opening before him: to marry Elizabeth himself, and to marry Lady Jane Grey to the young King Edward. Elizabeth played safe, and not only declined an offer of marriage, but also fought shy of the financial deals which he suggested to her. Whether she was fond of him or not is a matter of speculation, but she knew enough to realise that her position as sister to the King meant that any contract of marriage would require formal state approval, while anything other than that ran the risk of being construed as treasonable.

Thomas Seymour was arrested and charged with treason in January 1549, and it was at this stage that Elizabeth and her household came under close scrutiny. Sir Robert Tyrwhit, a special commissioner of the Council, was sent to question Elizabeth at Hatfield, while Kat Ashley and Thomas Parry were sent to the Tower. Tyrwhit records that he found Elizabeth 'marvellously abashed, and did weep tenderly a long time',[10] but she flatly refused to accuse her governess of lax behaviour and denied involvement with Seymour. Tyrwhit acknowledged the skill and cunning with which she met his questions, as she pressed for very specific aims — the restoration of her good name and the freeing of her servants from the Tower. So long as they were imprisoned and Lady Tyrwhit was in Kat Ashley's place, Elizabeth maintained, suspicion would still rest on her. She demanded that a proclamation of her innocence be made, and within a year she had both her servants back again. In December of the same year, she was received at court by her brother 'with great pomp and triumph'.

The trial of Seymour in 1549 tested all Elizabeth's powers of resilience and ability to manoeuvre. Tyrwhit expressed his surprise at her capabilities, and noted that there seemed to be an agreement between Elizabeth, Kat Ashley and Parry as to exactly what story they should all tell. Writing to the Protector in January 1549 at the start of his cross-examining, he noted her dislike of Lady Tyrwhit and added:

> she fully hopes to recover her old mistress again. The love she yet beareth her is to be wondered at. I told her if she would consider her honour and the sequel thereof, she would, considering her years, make suit to your Grace to have one, rather than to make delay to be without one one hour. She cannot digest such advice in no way; but if I should say my phantasy, it were more meet she should have two than one.[11]

Two governesses were needed, in his opinion, to control this tough-minded teenager who could sulk for days, wear people down with complaints and outclass a skilled interrogator by refusing to be pinned down. Many of the characteristics that came to public note later in her life were already clearly present at this time.

Thomas Seymour was executed in March 1549. Gregorio Leti quotes Elizabeth as having said of him that 'this day died a man with much wit and very little judgement', but this is doubtless as fictitious as the rest of Leti's documentation about Elizabeth. Nevertheless it has been frequently quoted, and might almost be said to serve as Seymour's epitaph. Less than a year later his brother, Edward Seymour Duke of Somerset, followed him to the block. Meanwhile, Elizabeth had emerged as the serious young academic, devoted 'sweet sister Temperance' to the young King and in favour again at court. With her reputation intact, she became a more prominent figure than she had done in the past. Chapuys wrote in January 1551 that she had been honourably received by the Council 'to show the people how much glory belongs to her who has embraced the new religion and is become a very great lady'.[12] She was beginning to build up her popularity as what Paul Johnson describes as 'a Protestant princess of striking appearance and notable accomplishments'.[13]

Elizabeth survived this first crisis and survived it well. The second great crisis of her life was potentially far more dangerous, and although she was older and more experienced, nevertheless it brought her close to the brink, as her letters show. The crisis began in the summer of 1553, with the lingering death of Edward VI. Next in line was Edward's sister Mary, but her ardent Catholicism provoked a powerful Protestant faction, led by the Duke of Northumberland, to alter the succession in favour of his daughter-in-law, Lady Jane Grey. Bishop Ridley proclaimed that both Mary and Elizabeth were bastards, and ratified Jane Grey's claim to the throne as a great-niece of Henry VIII. Elizabeth refused to co-operate with the Northumberland faction, and stayed closeted at Hatfield House during Jane's nine-day reign. When Northumberland's supporters deserted him and he was placed under arrest in the Tower, Elizabeth rode out to greet her sister Mary and hail her as Queen. However great the differences between the sisters might have been, both laid claim to the same father and through him to the succession. The only logical move for Elizabeth to make was to offer wholehearted support to the new Queen, regardless of religious differences.

Mary's accession caused major changes in Elizabeth's life. Firstly, and most fruitfully, it affirmed the right of Henry's daughters to the succession and set a precedent for a woman ruler. Secondly, Mary's tactics provided Elizabeth with a model of how *not* to rule, and it is probably safe to say that Mary's dogmatism and inflexibility served to strengthen Elizabeth's tendency towards a more fluid approach. In other words, while Elizabeth refused to be pinned down Mary increasingly boxed herself into tight corners from which she was unable to escape.

The frustrations of her life before her brother's death had left Mary little option but to cling tenaciously to her main source of comfort, the Church of Rome. She had seen her father divorce her mother and watched her mother die in a state of unhappiness and unfulfilment; she had suffered the humiliation of being declared a bastard and dispossessed in favour of a much younger sister; no marriage had been arranged for her, and — perhaps worst of all — she had seen the process of movement away from Rome towards a Protestant state accelerate beyond her worst imaginings. Once she became Queen, therefore, she saw herself as divinely inspired to carry out a mission — to bring back the growing numbers of heretics into the arms of the true Church, to restore her mother's good name and to make a Catholic marriage herself in order to provide the country with a Catholic heir. She seems to have been a serious woman, gentle with those around her and studious, and it is a bitter irony that she should be remembered across the centuries as 'Bloody Mary', whose mass burnings of those whose souls she wanted to save caused such revulsion that it only fuelled resistance instead of crushing it.

At Mary's coronation Elizabeth was given equal precedence with Anne of Cleves and for a short time relations between the sisters were formal but cordial. Then Mary began to insist on Elizabeth's attendance at Mass and her public demonstration of adherence to the Catholic faith. Elizabeth began her usual tactics of avoidance; she wept and said she had never had proper instruction in the old religion and asked for guidance, she complained of such pains when attending Mass that she was forced to leave and wore a replica of a miniature book containing the last prayer of her brother, a decidedly Protestant King. Her position became extremely difficult; she could not simply begin to practise Mary's religious rites, because she had become strongly associated with the Reformed Church movement. She must have realised that there was a strong chance of her becoming Queen if she could hold out long enough. Mary was in her late thirties, child-bearing would be difficult if not impossible, and she was in poor health. If Elizabeth had simply agreed to Mary's demands she would have lost all credibility in the country at large, and she kept a careful eye on her public reputation and base of future support. To agree to Mary's demands, therefore, would have meant losing the supportive base which was necessary to her future ambitions; not to agree meant that she ran the risk of being imprisoned or even executed for heresy.

Elizabeth's delaying tactics did not work. Relations between her and Mary deteriorated and by November 1553 the ambassador of Charles V, Simon Renard, was writing to his master about a conversation with the Queen in which he reiterated the advice given by others as well 'that it would be better to take Madame Elizabeth at once and confine her in the Tower'.[14] The French ambassador, writing to his master at the same time, noted that Elizabeth was so out of favour that none of the court ladies dared visit her in her room or even speak to her without the Queen's permission, and she now had to take a subordinate position at court to the Countess of Lennox and the Duchess of Suffolk. There was only one thing Elizabeth could do, and that was to plead to be allowed to leave. Permission was finally granted and Elizabeth left for her house at Ashridge in early December. As a gesture of friendship, Mary gave her a sable wrap, but the hostility and suspicion between the sisters was too close to the surface now to be disguised.

Mary had been proceeding with plans to marry Philip of Spain, although this idea was a source of considerable anxiety to many within the kingdom. Early in 1554 came the first uprising against the regime, a plot led by a group of Protestant noblemen to depose Mary and replace her with Elizabeth, who was to be married to Edward Courtenay; he was a direct descendant of the Plantagenet King Edward IV and had even been imprisoned for a time by Henry VIII because of the strength of his claims to the throne. The rebellion was crushed quickly, but the burning question became the need to determine what part, if any, Elizabeth had played in the plot. Mary and her Council were only too ready to believe that she had been deeply involved, and

Elizabeth was ordered to return to London for questioning.

Elizabeth sent back word that she was too ill to travel. The spate of executions of conspirators and others who might represent a danger to Queen Mary had begun in earnest; Lady Jane Grey, who had been imprisoned since Mary's accession, was beheaded in early February, along with her husband. The French ambassador to Scotland, Antoine de Noailles, wrote shortly afterwards that some of Mary's bravest and most gallant men were hanging from gibbets all over the country, while the prisons were crammed with prominent people and members of the nobility. Elizabeth, he writes, 'is so ill . . . that her life is despaired of'. She was swollen and exhausted, and there was fear that she had been poisoned. These symptoms point to some kind of nervous crisis, another of the neurotic maladies to which Elizabeth was particularly prone at this period of her life. De Noailles's letter concludes with a bleak picture of the state of the realm:

> there is no other news than that every day someone is condemned to death; this one has been executed; and yet another has been taken prisoner; in like manner, I foresee that all these events and others which would take too long to write to you, that matters are in a bad way . . . for this Queen, and are in a fair way to ruin this kingdom.[15]

Elizabeth was carried into London on a litter on 22 February, and she used the occasion to make people aware of her presence. She had her litter uncovered and lay exposed to public gaze, dressed completely in white and looking pale and ill. Once in London she was held at Whitehall, until three weeks later the summons came for her to be taken to the Tower.

The Tower was a place to be feared. Not only was it the prison to which traitors were sent and from which few emerged except to walk to the executioner's block, but it was dank, uncomfortable and cold. Throughout her life Elizabeth hated bad smells and closed environments; she was still taking long healthy walks in her old age and was always heavily perfumed. The prospect of any period of confinement during cold spring weather and immediately after a period of nervous illness must have been bad enough, but imprisonment in the Tower was the worst of all. When the news came Elizabeth tried one more delaying tactic; she insisted on writing a letter to the Queen, and spent so long doing it that the tide turned and her journey to the Tower had to be put off for one more day.

The letter from Elizabeth to Mary shows how terrified she was at that time. The handwriting so praised by Roger Ascham is scrawled and uneven; she filled only one sheet and part of another, and drew wavering diagonal lines across that second page so that nothing could be added by anyone bent on forgery.[16] In her letter Elizabeth reiterates her innocence and asks to be allowed to see Mary personally to plead her case; she cites instances of people who have been condemned because they were denied the chance to speak to the ruler: 'I have heard of many in my time cast away for want of coming to the presence of their Prince'. The example she gives is that of Thomas Seymour, but she must also have had in her mind the case of Catherine Howard, dragged screaming down the gallery at Hampton Court when refused access to Henry, or her own mother, Anne Boleyn, who is said to have held up Elizabeth as a baby in her arms to Henry looking down upon her from a window in Greenwich palace. Both women, mother and step-mother, had died on the block after failing to have direct contact with the King and thoughts of their deaths must have been in Elizabeth's mind. The letter concludes in a rush that reveals her panic; all Elizabeth's skill in stylistic composition has gone and instead there is an almost childlike determination to cram in statements of her innocence:

> Therefore, once again, kneeling with humbleness of heart, because I am not suffered to bow the knees of my body, I humbly crave to speak with your Highness, which I would not be so bold as to desire if I knew not myself most clear, as I know myself most true. And as for the traitor Wyatt, he might peradventure write me a letter, but on my faith I never received any from him. And as for the copy of the letter sent to the French King, I pray God confound me eternally, if ever I sent him word, message, token, or letter, by any means, and to this truth I will stand in till my death.

The next day was Palm Sunday. Word did not come back from the Queen, and Elizabeth made the journey by barge down the Thames in the rain to the Traitors' Gate. Her entry to the Tower has become a legend and according to John Foxe, the Protestant chronicler, she refused at first to go in and sat down in the rain announcing: 'Better sit here than in a worse place, for God knoweth, not I, where you will bring me'. She was taken, in fact, to the Bell Tower, a cold airless room with an adjoining garderobe and latrine. Here she remained for two months, continually in fear of the announcement of her impending execution, while from the walkway along which she was permitted to take some exercise she was aware of the executions of other inmates of the Tower taking place on Tower Hill.

While Elizabeth remained imprisoned and in fear of her life, the degree of Protestant resistance to Mary's policies was intensifying. It is paradoxical that though she was in the place of extreme danger Elizabeth was in fact becoming increasingly safe, as it became clear to Mary that her execution would have led to full-scale rebellion. Two months after her arrival at Traitors' Gate Elizabeth left the Tower, en route for the dilapidated palace of Woodstock where she was to be held, still a prisoner but out of the capital where there was such strong support for her cause. Her warden was Sir Henry Bedingfield, a staunch Catholic gentleman who was governor of the Tower and captain of the Queen's guards. Despite his serious, scrupulous sense of obedience to his superiors, a relationship of mutual respect developed between him and Elizabeth, who was quick to perceive that she might well be able to wear him down with her unpredictable behaviour and win privileges for herself. Her departure from the Tower must have given her a huge boost of self-confidence; not only had she escaped the place of imminent death, but as she left London people had cheered and thrown flowers and rung bells and at Wycombe she had been given so many cakes and breads that she had to ask people to stop because they could no longer be carried. This public assurance of her position in the country must have eased the fear of the previous months and restored a great deal of her strength of spirit. Imprisonment at Woodstock, though distasteful, was nothing like so frightening. Its chief disadvantage was the discomfort of the place, since the building was so dilapidated that only four rooms in the old gatehouse were fit for use. Elizabeth kept up a barrage of complaints about cold, damp, cramped conditions, lack of exercise, and illness; she demanded court doctors, the return of her own servants, permission to write letters and unlimited paper and ink. The solemn

Bedingfield endeavoured to do his duty by searching her laundry and banning unsuitable books, but, constantly harassed by Elizabeth, he found his position difficult. Later in life, Elizabeth used to refer to him affectionately as 'my gaoler' and stayed with him at his home in Norfolk in 1568, so whatever passed between them a bizarre kind of friendship seems to have developed.

On the cover of one book belonging to Elizabeth, an English translation of St Paul's Epistles, are embroidered in gold the words: 'Vincit omnia pertinax virtus E. C. [Elisabetha Captiva]'. The English translation is 'Tenacious virtue overcomes all' signed by 'Elizabeth, the Prisoner'. The expression gives a clue to her state of mind. Tenacity and insistence on her innocence were the keys to her freedom.

In July 1554 Philip of Spain landed in England and Mary's long hoped for marriage finally took place. By September there were rumours that she was pregnant, and when the birth of the child seemed imminent, in April 1555, Elizabeth was summoned back to London from Woodstock. Once in London she had an interview with Mary, which has been described (or invented) by Foxe, to whom we also owe the story of how Philip hid behind an arras to spy on the two women. This legend has been further developed by various novelists, who have constructed an imaginary passion on the part of Philip and Elizabeth, a passion which they would have us believe lay behind his desire to marry her immediately after Mary's death. In fact, what seems much more likely is that Philip put pressure on Mary to bring Elizabeth back to court not out of any sexual desire but out of political expediency. If Elizabeth provided a focal point for Protestant conspirators it would be far easier to watch her at court than in some obscure, poorly guarded country house. Moreover, plans were again under way for a marriage between Elizabeth and a suitable Catholic prince, and these could more easily be put into effect if Elizabeth were seen to be at court rather than under house arrest.

Mary's 'pregnancy' failed to bear fruit. The expected date of childbirth came and went, and Mary's swollen stomach began to deflate. She may have been suffering from a false pregnancy, or from a form of psychotic illness, or she may have had a tumour. Whatever the cause, the mental suffering must have been acute as all her hopes crumbled and her husband began to make plans to leave the country. Now in a state of despair, she refused to move the court for the summer and sat for hours on her cushions on the floor in complete silence, just as Elizabeth was to sit, half a century later, before she died. The court was crowded, sanitary conditions deteriorated and still Mary stayed on until, with the risk of plague now a real threat, she broke up the court and went out of the city. Shortly afterwards Philip left. De Noailles wrote that Spanish noblemen were leaving for Flanders after him every day, 'suspecting that their master's absence will not be a short one'. He also described how Elizabeth had attended Mass every day with the Queen, but that when Philip and Mary passed through London on their way to see Philip embark from Greenwich, Elizabeth had gone 'alone by water in a very badly-fitted boat, with only four ladies and two or three gentlemen, which has caused much discontent among the people'.[17]

With Philip gone and the pregnancy non-existent, Mary became introspective and her suspicions of her sister grew. She allowed Elizabeth to leave London for Hatfield, but could not act against her except in small ways, such as the sudden arrest of Kat Ashley in May 1556, for Philip had expressly requested Mary to treat Elizabeth with care, no doubt with the thought that she might be his future wife. He persuaded Mary to bring Elizabeth to Hampton Court for the Christmas of 1556, and when he returned to England in May 1557 he proposed that Elizabeth should marry his cousin, Emmanuel Philibert of Savoy, as part of his programme of building up the Habsburg–Tudor alliance. Elizabeth refused and was sent back to Hatfield in disgrace. A letter to Queen Mary from Sir Thomas Pope quotes Elizabeth as saying she was resolutely opposed to marriage: 'What I shall do hereafter I know not; but I assure you, upon my truth and fidelity, and as God be merciful unto me, I am not at this time otherwise minded than I have declared unto you; no, though I were offered the greatest prince in all Europe'.[18]

Elizabeth held out against marriage. When Philip left England again in June 1557 and Mary's hopes of a pregnancy collapsed for the second time, she must have realised that it was only a matter of time before she came to power in her sister's place. Certainly the foreign envoys to Mary's court were well aware of this possibility, and though Mary delayed until the very end before making Elizabeth her successor, those around her knew that she would eventually have to give way. The ambassador to the Doge

34

of Venice recounts how Mary kept insisting that Elizabeth was the daughter of a woman who had caused her and her own mother great pain, and even that Elizabeth was not Henry's daughter at all, but as Mary's last illness worsened pressure was put on her to name her sister as successor. Any other policy could bring about full-scale revolt, and the country was in a very insecure financial state, with powerful forces of discontent moving in various ways. Mary capitulated and named her sister. Early on 17 November 1558 she died, and by noon on the same day news had been brought to Elizabeth at Hatfield.

Waiting at Hatfield, Elizabeth had been deliberately careful. There was always the risk that she would be persuaded to go to London by the news of Mary's death, and that this would be simply a means of trapping her. She had told Sir Nicholas Throckmorton that she would need as evidence the betrothal ring from Mary's own hand, but when the lords of the Council themselves came to Hatfield to bring her the news, she knew that it must be true. She is said to have fallen on her knees and declared that 'this is the Lord's doing and it is marvellous in our eyes'. Whatever the problems of governing, and they were awesome in prospect, anything must have seemed better than the years of insecurity and imaginings. Elizabeth had said that the last months of Mary's life were like being buried alive, and her various illnesses show the strain she must have been living under. With Mary dead and huge popular support in the country, the wheel of fortune had finally revolved and left her at the top.

Notes

1. Frances Yates, *Astraea: The Imperial Theme in the Sixteenth Century* (London: Routledge & Kegan Paul, 1975), pp. 85–6.
2. Letter from Eustace Chapuys to Emperor Charles V, 10 September 1533, quoted in Frank A. Mumby, *The Girlhood of Queen Elizabeth* (London: Constable, 1909), p. 3.
3. Letter from Lady Bryan to Thomas Cromwell, 1536, quoted ibid., pp. 16–18.
4. Paul Johnson, *Elizabeth I: A Study in Power and Intellect* (London:

Weidenfeld & Nicolson, 1974), p. 11.

5. Letter attributed to Elizabeth by Gregorio Leti, quoted in Mumby, *Girlhood*, pp. 93–4.
6. George Ballard, *Memoire of British Ladies who have been celebrated for their writings or skill in the learned languages, arts and sciences* (London: T. Evans, 1775).
7. Letter from Roger Ascham to John Sturmius, 1550, quoted in Mumby, *Girlhood*, pp. 69–72.
8. MMC Salisbury MSS I i 65, *State Papers . . .*, ed. Samuel Haynes and William Murdin (London, 1740–57), I.
9. Letter from Elizabeth to Thomas Seymour, July 1548, repr. in G. B. Harrison, *The Letters of Queen Elizabeth*, (London: Cassell, 1935), p. 8.
10. *State Papers . . .*, I, p. 69.
11. Letter from Sir Robert Tyrwhit to the Protector Somerset, 19 February 1559, quoted in Mumby, *Girlhood*, pp. 54–5.
12. Letter from Eustace Chapuys to Emperor Charles V, January 1551.
13. Johnson, *Elizabeth*, p. 34.
14. Simon Renard to Emperor Charles V, 29 November 1553, quoted in Mumby, *Girlhood*, pp. 90–1.
15. Letter from Antoine de Noailles to M. D'Orsel, 21 February 1554, quoted ibid., pp. 107–8.
16. Facsimiles of this letter are reproduced ibid., fold-out between pp. 116–17 and in Neville Williams, *The Life and Times of Elizabeth I* (London: Weidenfeld & Nicolson, 1972), pp. 30–1.
17. Letter from Antoine de Noailles to the Queen-Dowager of Scotland, 9 September 1555, quoted in Mumby, *Girlhood*, pp. 200–1.
18. Letter from Sir Thomas Pope to Queen Mary, 26 April 1558, quoted ibid., pp. 236–8.

2 'This Virgin's Estate'

Biographers have been fond of depicting Elizabeth's accession in glowing colours. A youthful, energetic woman with a reputation for religious tolerance and a keen sense of justice had succeeded an ageing, embittered woman who through the cries of martyrs at the stake had lost her struggle to re-convert England to Roman Catholicism. Once on the throne Elizabeth proceeded to govern wisely and well and to encourage the flowering of the arts and sciences. Refugees returned, hope blossomed for the beleaguered Protestants of the Netherlands and Elizabeth became the focal point for the dawning of a new age. This is a pleasant vision, and obviously one which Protestant historians sought to encourage. William Camden, who produced the earliest history of her reign (the first part appeared in 1615, the remainder in 1625), declared that she was proclaimed Queen with 'happy acclamations and most joyfule applause of the people' and that 'neither did the people ever embrace any other Prince with more willing and constant mind and affection, with greater observance, more joy-full applause, and prayers reiterated whensoever she went abroad during the whole course of her life, than they did her'.[1] The Elizabethan age, the world of Good Queen Bess was, it seemed, about to begin. But in reality, the situation was rather different.

Elizabeth inherited a country on the verge of bankruptcy. One contemporary account of her problems lists them thus:

> The Queen poor, the realm exhausted, the nobility poor and decayed. Want of good captains and soldiers. The people out of order. Justice not executed. All things dear. Excess in meat, drink and apparel. Divisions among ourselves. War with France and Scotland, The French king bestriding the realm, having one foot in Calais and the other in Scotland. Steadfast enmity but no friendship abroad.[2]

Faced with this, Elizabeth had to act in a way that would be seen to be conciliatory. She already had a good relationship with William Cecil, whose influence over her became enormous as time went on, and she appointed him as Secretary of the Privy Council, a position that his son Robert eventually took over in 1596 towards the end of Elizabeth's reign. She aimed for a consensus government, carefully choosing her councillors to ensure some continuity from Mary's reign and to signal significant changes. A conservative in matters of religion, she never went as far as many Protestants might have wished. One typical move was her early Supremacy Bill, which accorded her the title of 'Supreme Governor' of the Church, rather than 'Supreme Head', a tactic designed to placate both Catholics and those Protestants who were uneasy about the idea of a woman claiming to be the head of the Church. By this move she gained the same powers over the Church as those enjoyed by her father, but stopped short of making a gesture that would have alienated some of her support. Careful, tactical thinking such as this coloured much of Elizabeth's policy in her early years, and served to create the image of tolerance that she so obviously sought to promote.

Abroad, the situation was problematic. One of the pressing needs of the new regime was to extricate England from conflicts on the Continent and to minimise the danger of a Franco-Scottish alliance that would squeeze England between its pincers. It is significant that the Scottish question should have been so important in Elizabeth's reign, and that her two greatest crises should have involved first Scotland, with the imprisonment and execution of Mary Queen of Scots, and then Ireland, with the rise and fall of the Earl of Essex. By policies which focused on the pre-eminence of England Elizabeth, like rulers before and after her, failed to understand the extent of the threat posed by the Scottish and Irish issues. Her policy, or failure to have a coherent policy in Ireland, sowed the seed for centuries of bloodshed to come. The Irish were perceived as barbarians, on the edge of civilisation, who could only be brought into line by brute force. That they were also Catholics increased the hostility towards them during the latter part of Elizabeth's reign. Scotland as an independent kingdom merged with England on Elizabeth's death, when James Stuart, son of Mary Stuart, became James I of England and James VI of Scotland, ruler of a united kingdom. London became increasingly the centre of power for the British Isles as a whole, and the importance of countries on the periphery of England was gradually marginalised.

Elizabeth's decision to appoint James as her successor came at the end of her life, but it had been expected for years. When James was born in 1566, the Scottish envoy to Paris wrote a poem proclaiming him as 'prince of Scotland, England, France and Ireland'. Through his mother, he claimed descent from Henry VII of England, and Mary's own claim to the English throne was the cause of the bitter struggle between herself and Elizabeth which culminated in her execution in 1587. But although James was widely perceived as the most obvious contender to succeed Elizabeth, for the first twenty years of her reign there was continued exploration of the possibility of Elizabeth producing her own heir. Elizabeth was therefore under considerable pressure to marry, and the urgency of finding her husband was summed up by William Cecil in a private letter to the Queen in 1560, in which she asked God to show her the way. He prayed continually, he said, 'that God would direct your heart to procure a father for your children and so shall the children of all your realm bless your seed. Neither peace or war without this will profit us long'.[3] Others prayed continually too. The Parliament of 1559 petitioned the Queen to marry as a matter of national security (as it also did in 1563). Elizabeth replied by declaring that ever since her 'years of understanding', she had decided to remain single. She made reassuring noises to the Commons, but stressed the force of her decision: 'But soe constant have I always continued in this determinatione — albeit my wordes and my youthe maye happily seeme hardlye to agree — that it is most trew I stand now free from any other meaning'. She concluded her speech with a prophetic statement: 'As for mee, it shall be sufficient that a marble stone shall declare that a Queene, having lived and reigned soe many yeeres, died a Virgine'.[4]

Elizabeth insisted on her right to remain single in terms that baffled her advisers and many onlookers, and which have interested commentators and biographers for centuries. Even Sir John Neale, whose biography of Elizabeth paints a glowing picture of her capabilities, discusses her refusal to marry in terms that can only be called patronising. He too falls into the trap of suggesting that the Seymour affair had somehow damaged her (he calls it 'her first cautionary tale') and that her decision should therefore be seen as deriving more from fear than from self-confidence. Certainly the interest in Elizabeth's marriage in the first years of her reign amounted to obsession. Doctors made statements about her ability to have children and her monthly periods — even her laundry was investigated for regular (or irregular) traces of menstrual blood. Both her contemporaries and those who have studied her life in later generations have sought rational explanations for behaviour that they deem to have been irrational. Among her contemporaries various rumours circulated to the effect that she did not have regular periods, that she was malformed, that she knew she was unable to have children. Others have speculated that Elizabeth's refusal to marry was the result of an emotional block which derived from the unfortunate experiences of marriage she had known in her life. All these assumptions have been based on the view that marriage is desirable and that without it a woman is unfulfilled.

It seems far more fruitful to approach the question from a different perspective. Elizabeth came to the throne at the age of twenty-five, when she had been of marriageable age for more than a decade. By sixteenth-century standards she was a mature woman, and becoming Queen finally gave her a chance to emerge from the coffin-like state she had endured in her early twenties during her sister's reign, and to express herself to the full. She had, finally, acquired power, and had moved from a position of powerlessness to one of total control. Had she married, she would have remained Queen but still have found herself in a subservient position to her husband, and she must have had strong feelings about the undesirability of that state of affairs. Her sister, married to a man who did not love her and was often away, had found her capacity to govern impaired by the depth of her personal misery. Elizabeth must have seen that in order to stay in control she needed to have a freedom of movement which depended upon emotional as well as physical independence.[5] As she observed the increasing disorder of Mary Stuart's life, beginning with one marriage to the vain, superficial Darnley in 1565 against all advice, and then two years later a second to the brutish Lord Bothwell, who was accused of her first husband's murder, Elizabeth must have been strengthened in her resolve not to risk being placed in a similar position.

The issue of marriage was a troublesome question in the sixteenth century. With the Reformation came another concept of the meaning of marriage and, paradoxically perhaps, it became

40

more difficult to obtain a divorce in Elizabeth's England than in previous centuries. The Church of England debated the divorce issue for decades, and finally came out against divorce completely in 1605. Moreover, in the hierarchical order of the pre-Reformation world virginity had been considered as a more exalted state than marriage. Now the new Protestant ethos, with its emphasis on the active rather than the contemplative life, placed a lower value on the virgin state and sought to promote the state of matrimony. It is as well to remember that in terms of property ownership and legal rights women were subordinated to their husbands in ways even more rigid than before, and with the suppression of the convents in England few options remained open to women except marriage.

In his interesting book *The Renaissance Notion of Woman* Ian Maclean suggests that there is one curious omission from Renaissance debates about women. Despite the fact that the great witch-burning craze raged through Europe from the late fifteenth century until the early seventeenth, he finds no discussion of sorcery relating to women. Puzzled by this, he suggests that 'the prosecution of widowed or single women as witches may be due also to an unspoken fear of abandoning the traditional view of woman as a person married or destined for marriage: this is consistent with suggestions already made about the institution of matrimony as a conservative influence on thought'.[6] If marriage is suddenly perceived as the ideal state of being for a woman, then women who stand outside that institution are immediately suspect. Yet in the Middle Ages, when single women, usually religious women, could rise to positions of great power (we need only think of St Catherine of Siena, who enjoyed high status in political and theological circles at a very young age, despite her apparent unwordliness and lack of training as a case in point) part of their authority arose from their unmarried state. Virginity was prized in ways that had already begun to disappear in Elizabeth's lifetime, and it is possible that she saw this with regret. Certainly her dislike of marriage went further than making sure it did not happen to her; she was strongly against clerical marriage and did her utmost to dissuade her maids-in-waiting from marrying. Elizabeth's rage when she found out that Robert Dudley, by then Earl of Leicester, had secretly married Lettice Knollys in 1576 was such that she was with some difficulty prevented from having them both arrested and placed in the Tower.

There were other reasons why Elizabeth may have refused to marry. The medieval convention of courtly love, with all its repressed sexuality and adoration of the lady, had re-emerged in the elaborate Renaissance courts, in a form more closely connected to intellectual game-playing than to metaphysics. Elizabeth enjoyed this game and played it well; she enjoyed being the object of desire without being possessed, and she must also have enjoyed arousing that desire and offering suggestions of fulfilment which both parties knew would never be met. As a queen, she could play the game on a much vaster scale, for now it could take on political dimensions too. When she came to the throne she was unquestionably the most attractive marriage proposition in Europe, and that was a position to be used to its best advantage. Suitors flocked to her court and she continued to offer herself as a potential bride for a good twenty years after coming to power, a tactic that, amazingly, continued to be taken seriously.

In her choice of advisers, Elizabeth surrounded herself with intellectual men bent on gaining power and property, and all older than she was. On her accession, however, various possibilities were presented to her that she had previously been denied. Within a very short time she had begun to exercise her right to enjoy those new prospects. The tone of her regime had been set by her coronation, which she appears to have delighted in, making gracious speeches of thanks, taking her time to watch the pageants performed in her honour, showing herself off in her robes of cloth of gold and smiling so often that the envoy of the Duke of Mantua commented that in his opinion she exceeded the bounds of gravity and decorum. Present at her coronation was her new Master of the Horse, a young man of her own age, Lord Robert Dudley.

The relationship between Elizabeth and Dudley went through various stages until his death in 1588. They often quarrelled, and when she thought he had taken too much power into his own hands during his mission to the Low Countries in 1586, she publicly rebuked him in a strongly worded letter:

We could never have imagined, had we not seen it fall out in experience, that a man raised up by ourself and extraordinarily favoured by us above any other subject of this land, would have in so incompatible a sort broken our commandment, in a cause that so greatly toucheth us in honour . . . and, therefore, our express pleasure and commandment is, that all delays and excuses laid apart, you do presently, upon the duty of your allegiance, obey and fulfil whatsoever the bearer hereof shall direct you to do in our name; whereof fail you not, as you will answer the contrary at your uttermost peril.[7]

That letter was written in February 1586. In July of the same year, she wrote an affectionate, chatty letter, which begins: 'Rob, I am afraid you will suppose by my wandering writings that a midsummer moon hath taken large possession of my brains this month, but you must needs take things as they come in my head, though order be left behind me'.[8]

These two letters, so utterly different in tone and content, symbolise in some respect the relationship between Elizabeth and Dudley. That she loved him seems beyond doubt. When he died in 1588, though she took no part in arranging his funeral, she placed his last letter to her in her private box and kept it close to her bed. But their relationship was not easy, and in his latter years Elizabeth seems to have treated him with a good deal of tolerance rather than respect. Dudley was very much an *arriviste*, a pushy man (Cecil disliked him intensely, and the feeling was mutual) given to womanising, and not averse to making shady deals at home and abroad in order to increase his personal wealth and status. He seems to have had great charm where women were concerned, and his life was punctuated with a series of scandalous liaisons with married and unmarried ladies of the nobility. He was strongly disliked by his fellows, however, and was the subject of savage satirical attacks by the public at large. A sensational book by an anonymous author published in 1584, *Leycester's Commonwealth*, accused him of seducing large numbers of women, murdering his rivals and being the most hated man in England. He was, it claimed, both a criminal and a lecher, 'overwhelmed and defamed in all vice'. The lurid language of this tract reveals how much Dudley was disliked and even though the more vivid claims can be discounted, it is a measure of his unpopularity that few bothered to refute the charges.

Despite this, Elizabeth loved him and heaped honours upon him from the start of their relationship. In his youth he was extremely handsome, he rode well, which Elizabeth admired, shared her passion for dancing and generally gave her the chance at last to enjoy the sensuality of life. Almost immediately, in the goldfish bowl of the court, gossip began to circulate. The Spanish ambassador wrote that it was common knowledge that Elizabeth and Dudley were lovers, and in the autumn of 1560 he wrote to the Duchess of Parma that Secretary Cecil was in despair about Elizabeth's affair with Dudley and was threatening to resign.

> He implored me for the love of God to remonstrate with the Queen, to persuade her not to utterly throw herself away as she was doing, and to remember what she owed to herself and her subjects. Of Lord Robert he said twice he would be better in paradise than here . . . He told me the Queen cared nothing for foreign princes. She did not believe she stood in any need of their support. She was deeply in debt, taking no thought how to clear herself, and she had ruined her credit in the city.[9]

De Quadra went on to add that Elizabeth and Dudley were 'thinking of destroying Lord Robert's wife'. She, he said, was very well and taking care not to be poisoned, but word had gone out that she was ill and likely to die. His letter paints an extraordinary picture of Elizabeth conspiring to have her lover's wife murdered, the country sinking deeper into economic crisis and the Queen only concerned with satisfying her own desires.

The authenticity of the letter is not in doubt, but that of Cecil's statements is questionable, to say the least. The general view now is that Cecil set these and similar rumours in motion so that the Queen would hear them and come to her senses; certainly he seems to have been deeply concerned that Elizabeth was compromising herself with a married man, a social inferior, and was dangerously close to breaking her own resolution and marrying him. Pressure began to be exerted on Elizabeth to give him up. Throckmorton informed her that Mary Queen of Scots had joked about Elizabeth marrying her horsemaster and Kat Ashley appealed to her directly to pull herself together.

The romance between Elizabeth and Dudley has provided generations of writers with rather meatier material than some of the other aspects of her life. Sir Walter Scott, in *Kenilworth*, immortalised Dudley's wife Amy Robsart as the innocent victim of immoral machinations, while others have seen her death as putting an end to all Elizabeth's hopes of happiness. For at the height of the affair between Elizabeth and Dudley, his wife was found dead with a broken neck at the foot of a flight of stairs. Even though she had been suffering from terminal cancer and could therefore have collapsed, falling to her death, rumours of murder swept the country. Elizabeth sent Dudley away from court to try and quell the gossip, but the damage was done. If she had ever been considering marriage to him, that prospect had to be dismissed. He, for his part, continued for some time longer to hope for marriage to Elizabeth, but the case against him was too strong. Elizabeth cared for her reputation above most other things, and she had the shrewdness to see that the death of Dudley's wife had created a crisis from which it would be difficult to extricate herself. To marry him with the memory of the death still in everyone's mind would be unthinkable. Nevertheless, she gradually restored him to favour, making him grants of property and placing him in an apartment adjoining her own with which, the Spanish ambassador reported, he was delighted.

Sifting through the mountain of hearsay evidence and speculation about Elizabeth and Dudley, what emerges is a sad rather than a shocking picture. Surrounded by ever-watchful courtiers, many of whom were hostile to her, under pressure from all sides to marry and ensure the safety of the realm by giving birth to children, isolated and moving through a maze of intrigue and patronising advice that often bordered on contempt, the few months of pleasure that Elizabeth was able to enjoy with Dudley in 1560 must have lifted her life on to another level. They had met years before, and had been imprisoned in the Tower at the same time, so they already shared common ground. Whether she seriously thought about marrying him or not, she did enjoy his company and the two of them rode, talked and played together in a way that she did not find possible with others. Dudley was highly educated, he was an extrovert, he was the patron of artists and writers of all kinds, he converted the old castle of Kenilworth into a magnificent palace, and when Elizabeth visited him there in 1575 he arranged for a display of tournaments, pageants and performances that was startlingly lavish even in that age of elaborate ceremonial events.

The hatred and envy that Dudley inspired made him a dangerous figure at Elizabeth's court. The possibility of marriage between them lingered on until 1564 when, in a gesture that has often puzzled commentators, Elizabeth offered Dudley as a prospective husband to Mary Queen of Scots. She announced to Sir James Melville, the Scottish envoy, that if she had been minded to take a husband, she would have taken Dudley, but since she was determined to end her life in virginity she was graciously offering him to her beloved fellow Queen. Mary firmly rejected this suggestion, but for a time at least Elizabeth did hold it out as an option. We can speculate as to whether she was serious or whether she was deliberately trying to provoke the Queen of Scots, whom she feared and disliked, into rushing into another disastrous marriage as an alternative to Dudley. That is precisely what Mary did, marrying Lord Darnley with fatal consequences for them both. Elizabeth had learnt that secret negotiations were already under way between Mary Stuart and Lady Lennox, Lord Darnley's mother, and on one occasion she openly accused Melville of preferring Darnley, whom she described as 'yonder long lad', to her own choice. Melville swiftly replied that any woman would be bound to prefer Lord Robert to such a lady-faced boy.

In 1562 Elizabeth contracted smallpox. The fear of this disease was so great that Elizabeth was at one stage deemed to be on her deathbed. The account of what happened during her illness comes from the Spanish ambassador de Quadra — not always an accurate reporter. He recorded that Elizabeth took the opportunity to make two significant statements about Dudley: firstly that nothing improper had ever passed between them, and secondly that in the event of her death he should become Protector of the Realm. What Cecil thought about this is not set down, but in any case Elizabeth recovered after a fortnight and, fortunately, was not disfigured by the disease. (Less lucky was Lady Mary Sidney, Dudley's sister and mother of the two great poets, Philip and Mary. She was badly marked by the smallpox as a result of nursing Elizabeth devotedly through the illness and contracting it herself.) If de Quadra is to be believed, therefore, on her supposed deathbed, Elizabeth had both declared her faith in Dudley's loyalty and capacity to rule and had also stated that their relationship was innocent.

There is little point in further speculation about whether

Elizabeth did or did not have a sexual affair with Robert Dudley. They obviously had a close relationship, a friendship that she valued greatly and that offered her possibilities that she could not find elsewhere. I find it equally feasible to believe that Elizabeth was wedded to the idea of virginity and opposed to marriage and that she may well have interpreted that idea of virginity metaphorically rather than literally. There is no way in which the twentieth century mind can fully penetrate the complexities of the Renaissance mind across the distance of time that divides us.

There were other men in Elizabeth's life besides Dudley. One of her great favourites was Sir Christopher Hatton, whose gradual rise in the court began in 1562 when he was in his early twenties. He may have met Elizabeth during the Christmas festivities in the Inner Temple, when he was a student official at the presentation of *Gorboduc* on 6 January. His rise was much slower than Dudley's and he gradually obtained various preferments until finally becoming Lord Chancellor in 1587. Bess of Hardwick suggested that Elizabeth had thrown herself at Hatton and that the basis of their relationship was sexual, but it seems rather to have been an ideal platonic friendship. Hatton did not marry, and continued to lavish praise and gifts on Elizabeth until his death in 1591. She favoured him more after Dudley's marriage to Lettice Knollys, which Elizabeth found unforgivable, but as that marriage soured, her sympathies for Leicester returned to the fore and for a while she continued her old game of playing one man off against the other.

Both Hatton and Dudley reacted negatively when Elizabeth began another prolonged courtship ritual in 1579 with the French Duke of Alençon. There had already been an earlier French courtship, with Alençon's elder brother the Duke of Anjou in 1570. These negotiations had collapsed, principally after Elizabeth's announcement that it was a matter of conscience for her that if she married the Duke he would not be allowed to hear Mass. She even went so far as to have the articles of marriage drawn up, but then procrastinated and announced that a condition of the marriage was the restoration of Calais, the last post of English dominance on French soil which had been lost by Mary Tudor. Since Calais was at that time to France rather what Gibraltar is today to Spain, such a request was bound to be rejected. Elizabeth had found a way out of yet another unwanted marriage.

Nevertheless, the political situation in Europe in 1571 was disturbing. The Ridolfi Plot to depose and kill Elizabeth and put Mary Stuart on the throne instead had been exposed, but it was deeply worrying to see the extent of antagonism towards Elizabeth in Europe generally. In October the Spanish won a great victory at Lepanto, and the prospect of Spain's increasing power must have made Elizabeth think again about the advantages of a French marriage alliance. Then in 1572 came the full-scale slaughter of French Huguenots during the infamous St Bartholomew's Day Massacre. Elizabeth received the French ambassador with her court in full mourning (after keeping him waiting for a month) and wrote to Sir Francis Walsingham that he should point out to the French King the anomaly of trying to destroy Protestants while angling for a Protestant queen as bride for his brother:

> And therefore if that Religion of itself be so odious unto him that he thinks he must root out all the professors of it, how should we think his brother a fit husband for us, or how should we think that the love may grow, continue and increase betwixt his brother and us, which ought to be between the husband and the wife.[10]

Negotiations between the two countries lapsed for a time but were revived in 1578, the prospective husband now, as we have seen, the younger brother of Anjou, the Duke of Alençon. This time the marriage game took on a more ridiculous note. Elizabeth was forty-five, her prospective husband twenty years younger. He was much smaller than she was and reputed to be hideously ugly and badly disfigured by smallpox. Cecil, who seems never to have lost hope of Elizabeth's marriage, seriously insisted that Elizabeth might not be past child-bearing age and that women older than she had brought healthy children into the world. Elizabeth seems to have enjoyed Alençon's company, and nicknamed him her Frog. Lavish gifts were exchanged, and when he left England after a brief courtship visit, Alençon showered Elizabeth with passionate letters.

Whether Elizabeth was seriously interested in Alençon, or whether his arrival enabled her to get over her rage at the discovery of Dudley's marriage, is a matter for speculation. What is clear is that once again she was not allowed her own choice in the matter and was subjected to heavy pressure against the marriage from all directions. The St Bartholomew's Day Massacre had left a lasting antipathy for the French in the minds of many English Protestants, and Elizabeth's contemplation of a French marriage was seen to be as repugnant as her sister's choice of a husband from the other arch-enemy, Spain. Sir Philip Sidney wrote Elizabeth a letter explaining how he and others felt; since he had actually been in Paris at the time of the massacre he was speaking from first-hand knowledge. Then John Stubbs, a Puritan lawyer and country gentleman who later became a Member of Parliament, wrote and published a pamphlet entitled *The Discovery of a Gaping Gulf whereunto England is like to be swallowed by another French marriage if the Lord forbid not the bans by letting her Majesty see the sin and punishment thereof.* The title of the pamphlet gives the key to its content. It depicted the ageing Queen as a victim of deception. She was known to be too old to bear children and could risk death in the process, moreover Alençon was suffering from venereal disease, the punishment for having lived an immoral life. Alençon was proposing to bring a swarm of French scum across the Channel to leech off English wealth and Elizabeth, like a foolish old maid, was disposed to allow this to happen.

The publication of Stubbs's pamphlet sent Elizabeth into a rage. That she often lost her temper is well documented, but she had a particular hatred of scurrilous misogynous pamphlets. She had always detested John Knox, whose *Trumpet Blast against the Monstrous Regiment of Women* had infuriated her when it had appeared in 1558, even though Knox protested that it had been intended specifically for Mary Stuart and Marie of Guise, her mother. Elizabeth took exception to puritanical attacks on the capacity of women to rule, and Stubbs's pamphlet seems to have angered her in the extreme. She had Stubbs, his printer and his publisher all arrested and thrown in the Tower. She then endeavoured to have them hanged, and when this proved legally impossible she decreed that they should all lose their right hands. The printer was pardoned, but on the other two men the sentence was carried out. Before a silent crowd which disapproved strongly of Elizabeth's judgement, Stubbs had his hand cut off, after which he waved his hat in the air with his remaining hand, cried 'God save Queen Elizabeth!' and fell down in a dead faint. His companion, no less bravely, shouted that he had left on the block a 'true Englishman's hand'. The strength of public opinion against her after this, combined with the overall opposition to the marriage from her Council, forced Elizabeth to back down. If she had ever intended to marry Alençon, it was all over by the end of 1581. Even Cecil had now turned against the idea, and in view of the growing crisis in the Low Countries there seemed little point in continuing to irritate Spain with the prospect of an Anglo-French alliance. Elizabeth was unwilling to commit England to full-scale involvement in the struggle of the Protestant Low Countries against the Spaniards, and the French steered a careful course that left room for doubt and negotiation with both sides. When Alençon had finally left England, all his hopes of marrying Elizabeth gone, the Spanish ambassador quotes her as having said that: 'An old woman like me has something else to think about besides marrying; the hopes I gave that I would marry Alençon were given for the purpose of getting him out of the Netherland States; I never wished to see them in the hands of the French'.[11]

Before Alençon left he was given a large sum of money, negotiated in the form of a loan to enable him to continue his fight against the Spaniards. Elizabeth declared herself to be broken-hearted, and whatever the truth of her feelings she did put some of them down in a poem which shows an uneasy state of mind. Although Alençon may have been small, ugly and undesirable, he was still the last chance of marriage, the last suitor with whom she could play her favourite game of promising and refusing. When he left she was in her late forties and middle age was well advanced. Moreover, whether she had wanted him or not was not really the question; the fact was that once again she had been forced to conform to a set of expectations imposed upon her from without, and in the process she had been publicly ridiculed as a love-starved old maid. Her poem is couched in conventional expressions of sentiment, but the first verse has a note of honesty that I feel points to the deep frustrations she must have felt had come to a head in her life:

> I grieve and dare not show my discontent,
> I love and yet am forced to seem to hate.

I do, yet dare not say I ever meant,
I seem stark mute but inwardly do prate.
I am and not, I freeze and yet am burned,
Since from myself another self I turned.[12]

Notes

1. William Camden, *Annales, or the History of the Most Renowned and Victorious Princesse Elizabeth, Late Queen of England*, 4th edn (London: R. Bentley, 1688, repr. New York: AMS Press, 1970). Camden's account of the accession, in abridged form, is included in Richard Greaves (ed.), *Elizabeth I, Queen of England* (Lexington Mass., Toronto and London: D.C. Heath, 1974) pp. 3–11.
2. Quoted in Conyers Read, *Mr. Secretary Cecil and Queen Elizabeth* (London: Jonathan Cape, 1955), p. 124.
3. Letter from William Cecil to Queen Elizabeth, 21 June 1560, quoted ibid., p. 185.
4. Sir John Hayward, *Annals of the first four years of the reign of Queen Elizabeth* (London: Camden Society, 1840), pp. 32–3.
5. In a letter to King Eric of Sweden dated 25 February 1560, Elizabeth states explicitly that 'we shall never accept or choose any absent husband, how powerful and wealthy a Prince soever', reprinted in G.B. Harrison, *The Letters of Queen Elizabeth* (London: Cassell, 1935), pp. 31–2.
6. Ian Maclean, *The Renaissance Notion of Woman* (Cambridge: Cambridge University Press, 1980), pp. 88–9.
7. Letter from Elizabeth to Robert Dudley, Earl of Leicester, 10 February 1586, repr. in Harrison, *Letters*, pp. 174–5.
8. Letter from Elizabeth to Robert Dudley, Earl of Leicester, 19 July 1586, repr. ibid., pp. 178–9.
9. Letter from de Quadra, quoted in Read, *Mr. Secretary Cecil*, p. 200.
10. Letter from Elizabeth to Sir Francis Walsingham, 28 September 1572, repr. in Harrison, *Letters*, pp. 112–4.
11. Quoted in Frederick Chamberlin, *The Sayings of Queen Elizabeth* (London, Bodley Head, 1923), pp. 95–6.
12. 'On Monsieur's Departure', in Leicester Bradner (ed.), *The Poems of Queen Elizabeth I* (Providence, Rhode Island: Brown University Press, 1964), p. 5.

3 The Faerie Queen

Elizabeth's coronation procession, which took place in January 1559, was a great public display both of the people's expectations of their new Queen and of Elizabeth's ability to appeal directly to the masses. The machinery of modern government and policing works essentially in secret; committees meet behind closed doors, decisions are taken by small elite groups, rules are made and transformed into law by the few for the good of the many. All kinds of complex processes combine to ensure the strength of the state. By the end of Elizabeth's reign the basis for that kind of government had already been laid, not only in England but throughout Europe. When she first came to power, however, the principles of government were still very much medieval, where the key was the visibility of the processes of law enactment and enforcement rather than otherwise. In the lengthy changeover from a state ruled by a fighting monarch (Henry VIII had gone into battle at the head of his army, as had his Plantagenet predecessors) to one governed by a Parliament with a reigning rather than a ruling monarch, the apparatus of government became more and more complex and therefore less evident. In the early years of her reign Elizabeth showed herself regularly to the people in elaborate processions, progresses and state and religious rituals, a living symbol of government. She continued the tradition of laying hands on the sick to cure the King's Evil (a practice finally discontinued by the Hanoverian Kings). Her style, in effect, was deliberately theatrical and it is perhaps appropriate that the great renaissance of English theatre began during her reign.

Accounts of the coronation procession stress the way in which Elizabeth interacted with what went on around her, making witty remarks to performers in the many pageants, thanking people again and again for their prayers and good wishes, making speeches in English and in Latin. When she enquired about the meaning of one particular pageant and was told it represented Time, she replied: 'Time? How is that possible, seeing it is time that hath brought me hither'. And when an old man was seen to weep, she quickly remarked that it must be for joy. Accepting rich gifts and purses of gold, she also collected bunches of flowers and branches of rosemary and was careful to publicly proclaim her religious tendencies: 'a Bible in English richly covered was let down unto her by a silk lace from a child that represented Truth. Shee kissed both her hands, with both her hands shee received it, then shee kissed it; and lastly held it up, thanking the City especially for that gift, and promising to be a diligent reader thereof'.[1]

The Coronation was therefore a studied public display of good will and good intentions. Elizabeth was setting out from the beginning to be perceived as the people's Queen, and the phrase 'my people' was one that came readily to her lips throughout her reign. Nevertheless, apart from all this public show designed to reassure and heal some of the old wounds inflicted on the country during the Marian years, it was difficult to predict quite how Elizabeth would turn out as a ruler. When she came to the throne she was twenty-five years old, but had never really allowed her personality to flower. Even her tastes were unknown, since she had taken such pains to appear as the serious, devout bluestocking against whom complaint would be difficult. Effectively an unknown quantity, a cipher, she certainly had great skill in verbal manoeuvring and a natural inclination towards politics.

Wallace MacCaffrey, an American historian whose work on Elizabeth is coloured by a sexist approach, notes the sharp differences between her style and that of her father, brother and sister. He points out that she did not have any strong religious devotion, nor did she have Henry's 'zest for theological disputation', and she certainly had no interest in making a marriage alliance that would give England a larger voice in European affairs. He suggests that her lack of dynastic and personal ambition 'left a kind of vacuum in her political attitudes since they were not oriented toward the usual goals of action'.[2] This aspect of Elizabeth's character must have caused a great deal of perplexity at the start of her reign, since it posed an additional difficulty to the already huge problem of her sex. Sir John Neale has pointed out that 'government was a masculine business'[3] and that in purely practical terms the royal household was a male community of some 1,500 residents, with very few women other than maids-of-honour, girls of good families finishing their education, and menial servants. The machinery of the court, the steps up the ladder of preferment, the rituals and symbols of tradition were all primarily masculine. Throughout her life Elizabeth had to struggle against ambiguous attitudes towards women, attitudes that perceived women as intellectually and indeed intrinsically inferior, but she kept up the struggle with hard determination. One of the best examples of her public statements of her rights and abilities as a woman ruler is the speech she made to Parliament in 1566 when pressure on her to marry had become intolerable.

She informed them that she would marry when she chose to do so, and that she would only marry someone suitable to both her and the country. She reminded them of what had happened during Mary's reign, and declared: 'I will marry as soon as I can conveniently, if God take him not away with whom I mean to marry, or myself, or else some other great let happen'.[4] This is a typical piece of Elizabethan rhetoric; on the one hand she announces her intention to do something, while on the other she announces that she still has the right not to do it if her terms are not met. Central to the whole speech is a passage that has been frequently quoted, and which can be seen as a powerful statement of her own position:

Was I not born in this Realm? Were my parents born in any foreign country? Is there any cause that I should alienate myself from being careful over this country? Is not my Kingdom here? Whom have I oppressed? Whom have I enriched to other's harm? What turmoil have I made to this Commonwealth that I should be suspected to have no regard of the same? How have I governed since my Reign?

After this passionate series of questions, she built up to her conclusion:

As for mine own part, I care not for death, for all men are mortal. And though I be a woman, yet I have as good a courage, answerable to my place, as ever my father had. I am your anointed Queen. I will never be by violence constrained to do anything. I thank God I am endued with such qualities that if I were turned out of the Realm in my petticoat I were able to live in any place in Christendom.

At the end of her speech, it was noted that the House was stunned into silence. When Elizabeth put her full weight into safeguarding herself, she was always able to crush the opposition.

Her defence on this occasion was both personal and political. She reiterated not only the arguments against a foreign husband, but also her divine right as a monarch and her right as a woman to respect for her wishes. The speech is a tough one, an example of plain speaking that barely conceals the anger beneath its polite surface. The contemptuous comment that she would be able to survive anywhere in Christendom if turned out in her petticoat shows that she still had a sense of humour, despite feeling that she had been abominably treated by the men of Parliament complaining about her refusal to choose a husband.

It is quite likely that even without a kingdom Elizabeth would still have been a woman of striking achievement. Historians have tended to focus on her political sense (and frequently on their opinion of her inadequacies) while novelists have focused on her love life, but it seems to me that one of the most important keys to an understanding of Elizabeth's personality lies in the evidence we have of the way in which her intellectual and artistic tastes developed during her lifetime. For if Renaissance man, according to Castiglione[5] and other theoreticians of ideal behaviour, were a multi-faceted being trained in a wide variety of skills and accomplishments, so did this hold true for Renaissance woman. We have already seen how Elizabeth's early education trained her in the domestic arts as well as classical scholarship, in modern languages and needlework, in handwriting and theology. When she came to the throne she was at last able to exercise her right to develop in ways that she could choose herself: the unadorned black velvet dresses with no jewellery disappeared; witnesses remarked on the weight of magnificent rings she wore on her hands, while her apparent distaste for music evaporated as she presided over a musical renaissance in her court. As scholar, artist and patron of the arts and sciences, Elizabeth was remarkable, and she could not have combined that part of her life with the hard work of government without reserves of energy and determination not to give up activities which she enjoyed and needed for self-fulfilment.

It is perhaps not surprising, given the great flowering of English poetry that took place during Elizabeth's reign, that

Elizabeth should also have written poetry. In 1892 Ewald Flügel gathered together Elizabeth's writings and verse, but it was the American scholar Leicester Bradner who carefully examined the poems and questioned the authenticity of some of them.[6] Bradner's edition of Elizabeth's poetry and translations, published in 1964, divides her work into three categories — verse translations, poems of undoubted authorship and poems of doubtful authorship. Into this third category comes one of the most famous of all those poems attributed to her, the four-line reply she is reputed to have given to the priests who examined her during Mary's reign:

> Christ was the Word that spake it;
> He took the bread and brake it,
> And what the Word did make it
> That I believe and take it.

Although this poem probably circulated fairly widely (and was based on a verse by St Thomas Aquinas in the first place) there is considerable doubt about it having originated from Elizabeth although the ambiguous word-play is certainly typical of the kind she would have enjoyed. Bradner lists six poems as definitely by Elizabeth, one of which is the famous piece written on a window at Woodstock with a diamond:

> Much suspected of me,
> Nothing proved can be,
> Quoth Elizabeth prisoner.

The six poems are not literary masterpieces by any means, but they share certain significant features. They are all short — one poem entitled 'On Fortune' is only two lines, and the two longest, 'The Doubt of Future Foes' and 'On Monsieur's Departure' are of sixteen and eighteen lines respectively. What is most striking about the poems is the content. All are concerned with suspicion, false accusation, concealment and the shifting wheel of fortune. Most were written early in her life, though the two longest were probably written in two separate moments of crisis: 'The Doubt of Future Foes in 1569/70 after Mary Queen of Scots, described in line 11 as 'the daughter of debate', had fled to England, and 'On Monsieur's Departure' in 1582 when the marriage negotiations with France collapsed. Bradner has serious doubts about this latter poem, which he feels is far too explicit to be an authentic work by Elizabeth, but notes that it is generally held to be hers.

The poems are energetic and give the impression of having been written in moments of great emotion. They share the themes of insecurity and the instability of human plans. We can deduce from these poems, I feel, that Elizabeth occasionally used verse to express certain complex thoughts running through her own mind, but that her natural inclination was much more to prose rhetoric, to the quick reply, the crafted speech, the oratorical *tour de force*.

The theme of fortune is also dominant in her more extensive translation work. She prided herself on her translations and continued to work on them throughout her lifetime. Her version of Boethius's *De Consolatione Philosophiae* was written in 1593 when she was sixty, and her versions of Horace's *Ars Poetica* and Plutarch's *Moralia* date from five years later, in 1598. All her life she maintained a keen interest in the classics, in keeping with the education she had received in her youth, and she seems to have made great efforts to keep her knowledge alive. The translations were made at great speed, and notes on the manuscripts indicate that the Boethius was translated in less than a month. Her syntax is awkward, making the poem quite difficult to read, and from this we can see that in common with Renaissance scholars she favoured the method of literal translation, following in the foot-steps of the original author, to use a favoured metaphor of Elizabethan translators.

From Elizabeth's literary output we can make certain assump-tions. Firstly, she saw herself not only as a patron but also as a creator of the arts, and although her greatest skills were in oratory and in music, she nevertheless viewed her translation work as an important part of her life well into old age. Secondly, she seems to have chosen texts for their content, for the way in which the material could complement her own thoughts and feelings about particular situations. Her choice of Boethius, for example, is an interesting one. Boethius had fascinated genera-tions of writers — including Chaucer who also translated the *De Consolatione Philosophiae* — as much for his biography as for his writing. Imprisoned by the ruler he had served loyally for many years, Boethius was tortured and finally executed. He wrote his

57

great work while in prison and for the Middle Ages and the Renaissance he came to symbolise the ingratitude of princes; having been raised up to the highest, he was cast down to the lowest. The fickleness of fortune was an image always close to Elizabeth's heart and in the mid-1590s with England experiencing the worst economic recession of her reign, the war in Ireland accelerating and the court full of 'discontent and factions', as the French envoy reported, she must have had cause to think hard about the changing fortunes of the world in which she was growing old. In 1601, when she had Essex executed for treason after his years as rising star at the court, the idea of the fickleness of fortune must have returned to her, though we have no texts from that time. During her last five years, Elizabeth neither wrote nor translated poetry. The translation from Horace of 1598 dwells on old age, while the translation from Plutarch dwells on the ugliness of sycophants and flatterers. There is a sense of bitterness in these texts which I feel shows how carefully Elizabeth chose writers and works whose mood matched her own. The boldness of the young woman who scrawled verses on a window-pane had changed into the cynicism of an older woman who knew from experience the ways of the world and the corruption of the court.

Writing seems almost to have been a game that she played at certain crucial moments. Of greater importance to her was music, singing, playing and especially dancing. Edmond Bohun gives an account of how she spent her time when living at Richmond:

> Six or seven galliards of a morning, besides music and singing, were her ordinary exercise. . . . First in the morning she spent some time at her devotions, then she betook herself to the dispatch of her civil affairs, reading letters, ordering answers, considering what should be brought before the council and consulting with her ministers. . . . When she had thus wearied herself she would walk in a shady garden or pleasant gallery, without any other attendants than a few learned men; then she took coach and passed, in the sight of her people, to the neighbouring groves and fields, and sometimes would hunt and hawk; there was scarce a day but she employed some part of it in reading and study.[7]

A day such as this shows the restlessness and high energy of

Elizabeth's pattern of life. She always had a passion for hunting and for walking, obviously enjoying those hours when she could get out of the crowded court chambers, but the detail of her starting her day with dancing shows exactly how important this was to her.

Elizabethan dancing was a complex affair, involving the dancer in learning many different steps and performing considerable feats of agility. The galliard, for example, required the dancers to leap in the air and touch feet together, and there is a nice cameo of the 69-year-old Elizabeth sitting next to the French ambassador and watching her maids-of-honour dancing: 'In her youth she danced very well . . . when her maids are dancing she follows the time with her head, hand and foot. She rebukes them if they do not dance to her pleasure, and without doubt she is an expert. She says she used to dance very well when young; after the Italian manner of dancing high'.[8]

Elizabeth's skill in dancing was often used to impress visitors. When Sir James Melville came to court on a mission from Scotland in 1564 Elizabeth staged an impressive display, and then apparently confronted the Scottish envoy and demanded to know whether she or his mistress, Mary Queen of Scots, danced the best. Melville tactfully informed Elizabeth that Mary 'danced not so high and disposedly as she did', which was probably true if all the accounts of Elizabeth's grace and agility are to be believed. And although she ceased to dance in public when too old to create the same kind of impression, she is reported to have been seen by a visitor to Hampton Court who glanced through a window, dancing alone to whistle and tabor, with only her attendant Lady Warwick in the room. The idea that she could still have wanted to dance in her late sixties, and still tried out steps and enjoyed doing so gives an insight into the strength of her will and the depth of her passion. Some biographers have seen this incident as a pathetic picture of the ageing Queen prancing like a crazy old woman in the privacy of her chamber. I prefer to see it as a sign of the enthusiasm she still felt and still wanted to express. A contemporary Polish writer, Anna Pawlikowska-Jasnorzewska, writes about her own old age in terms of defiance; one of her poems talks about a grey-haired woman running on the beach, past amazed onlookers, insolently. I like to think of Elizabeth dancing insolently, in despite of the next generation performing their new steps and the peeping Toms spying in at her windows.

Besides dancing, Elizabeth is said to have composed ballads and songs, following the example of her father who composed Masses and motets. Henry VIII was also a skilled virginals player, and both his daughters were taught well and became proficient. Under Henry, the greatest influence on music came from France, while under Elizabeth Italy became the source of inspiration. Elizabeth had some sixty musicians in her service, which included the singers of the Chapel Royal and the instrumentalists of the Queen's Musick. Her interest in music involved both secular and religious forms; during her reign the madrigal emerged as an extraordinarily popular form, and one of the greatest exponents of this new Italian music was Thomas Morley, who in 1601 produced *The Triumphs of Oriana*, a collection of madrigals by over twenty composers, in honour of Elizabeth.

There were times, however, when aesthetic considerations gave way to larger political issues. John Dowland, the great composer and singer of lute music, was a favourite in the Dudley–Essex circle but was never granted a position in the Queen's service despite his obvious talent. The reason for this was that Dowland had converted to Roman Catholicism, and it was not until long after Elizabeth's death, when Dowland had recanted and returned to the Anglican faith, that he was finally granted a place at court in the service of James VI.

The question of music and religion was an important one for Elizabeth. With the dissolution of the monasteries had come the end of many choirs trained in church music, and with the abolition of the Latin rite much of the earlier music also became obsolete. The task of creating a new music for a new Church was therefore an important one, and one that Elizabeth seems to have taken very much to heart. Her two principal musicians employed in this task were Thomas Tallis and William Byrd, who dedicated their *Cantiones Sacrae* to the Queen in 1575. This work, presented in the seventeenth year of Elizabeth's reign, includes seventeen compositions in her honour, and the dedication praises both her elegant singing voice and her performance skills. Both Tallis and Byrd were religious conservatives; Byrd was frequently cited as a Catholic recusant though never actually prosecuted. During his lifetime Byrd wrote pieces that were used in the

English Church; he also composed Masses, but these were only published posthumously. That he could compose music for both Churches, and indeed was the composer of the famous Great Service of the Church of England, shows how flexible religious attitudes could be even in an age when religion was a life-or-death matter.

The case of Dowland reveals another aspect of the Elizabethan court scene. Although not given a position by Elizabeth, Dowland received support and patronage from Robert Dudley, and Dudley's role as a patron of the arts is indeed an impressive one. As Earl of Leicester he was a strong supporter of the theatre, and patron of the first actors' company, the Earl of Leicester's Men, established in 1574. The royal patent granted on 10 May 1574, which was to serve as a model for later patents, authorises five actors, including Shakespeare's renowned James Burbage:

> servauntes to oure trustie and welbeloved Cosen and Counsey-llor the Earle of Leycester, to use, exercise, and occupie the arte and facultye of playenge Commedies, tragedies, Enterludes, stage playes, and other such like as they have alredie used and studied, or hereafter shall use and studye, as well for the recreation of oure lovinge subjects, as for oure solace and pleasure when we shall thincke good to see them. . . .[9]

Later on Elizabeth had her own company, the Queen's Company, formed in 1583 by the orders of Sir Francis Walsingham, who took twelve of the finest actors from several other companies and swore them in as the Queen's servants, granting them wages and livery as grooms of the chamber. In 1600 alone she saw eleven plays performed.

Elizabeth seems to have enjoyed public spectacle and, as a woman of the Renaissance, she was able to derive pleasure from plays, from learned disputations, from sports such as bear- and dog-baiting that twentieth-century sensibilities would find barbaric. She had a Master of the Bears, and a bear pit on the South Bank was her personal property. Someone who took such pains to stage her own public appearances so carefully would be likely to admire the performances of others trained in the art. At a performance of Richard Edward's *Palamon and Arcite* at Oxford in 1566 a special door was cut in the wall to enable Elizabeth to go from her lodging to her seat facing the stage and make a splendidly theatrical entrance that perhaps upstaged the actors.

We have a fairly detailed account of one of her visits to the universities, a visit to Cambridge in 1564. Elizabeth arrived lavishly dressed, made speeches and joked with officials, attended special lectures, listened to sermons, saw *Aulularia* by Plautus, *Dido* and *Ezechias* performed in English. She enjoyed the visit so much that she postponed her departure for a day, though on the last evening she declined to attend a student production of a Sophoclean tragedy on the grounds that she was too tired. The visit provides an insight into the kind of entertainments she enjoyed, and her participation in the various activities shows how far she may be considered as a performer rather than as a passive spectator. However, her sense of humour and good will had its limits; when some of the students followed her to the next stage of her journey to perform a work which her busy schedule had not allowed her time to see, she lost her temper publicly. The piece was an anti-Catholic satire and included a scene of a dog with the Host in its mouth; Elizabeth swore and left the room, abandoning the players to perform to themselves.

Other productions occasioned royal anger too, such as the performance of William Shakespeare's *Richard II* in 1601. The day before Essex led his rebellion, his supporters arranged for a special performance of the play, originally written in 1597. With its theme of the deposition of a monarch the play was politically contentious, and Elizabeth was in no doubt as to its significance. She was predictably infuriated, and informed William Lambarde, Keeper of the Records in the Tower, that she knew well that she was supposed to be Richard — 'I am Richard II. Know ye not that?' She must also have been aware of the large number of plays appearing in the last decade of her reign in which the problem of kingship and of a state in crisis was explored and developed.

Though Elizabeth patronised the theatre, and obviously enjoyed poetry and music, her record as a patron of poets is not outstanding. Despite the works written in her honour she never gave preferment to John Lyly, whose *Euphues, The Anatomy of Wit* inspired a whole school of writing, nor did she offer much to Edmund Spenser, one of the greatest poets of the age. She seems to have been most interested in the advancement of learning, fascinated by the new philosophy and scholarship, by work in astronomy, geography, cartography and philosophy. In 1564 Dr John Dee, her astrologer and mathematician, was appointed Royal Adviser in mystic secrets, including alchemy, and she frequently visited Dee at his home in Mortlake where he kept his laboratory and the second largest private library in Western Europe, consisting of more than 4,000 volumes. Dee, whose contribution to Renaissance thought has been assessed very highly by Frances Yates[10], had taught science to Robert Dudley and was therefore also part of the intellectual circle around the Earl of Leicester, which included Sidney, Raleigh and Dyer.

Dee's work in astrology and alchemy led his opponents (particularly John Foxe) to condemn him as a conjurer, and biographers of Elizabeth often feel the need to excuse her apparent frivolity in dabbling in such enterprises. Even Paul Johnson offers the hypothesis that 'what we would today term the superstitious side of Dee's work made the least appeal to her'.[11] But to take this view is to ignore the significance of magic in the Renaissance world. Today we categorise and divide, placing the 'rational' sciences on one side, the 'irrational' on another, but in Elizabeth's England such a division would have been absurd. Dee's mathematical skills were remarkable and he was highly regarded throughout Europe; he was consulted not only as an astrologer but also as a cartographer, assisting with the preparation of charts for men such as Frobisher and Drake. Moreover, alchemy was taken very seriously. The Emperor Rudolph II of Bohemia assembled a large number of alchemists around him in Prague, as did a number of other European rulers. Some indication of the gravity which politicians and rulers accorded to alchemy can be found in an exchange of letters between Cecil, Lord Burghley, and envoys in Bohemia in 1588 (the year of the Spanish Armada) and immediately afterwards.

Dr Dee had been living in Bohemia, working with his associate Edward Kelley, who had been knighted by Rudolph II for his alchemical work. Dee returned to England in 1587 but Kelley remained, and the gist of the letters from Burghley involves the belief that Kelley possessed a powder that could transform base metals into gold. Burghley first pressed Kelley to return to England and work solely for the Queen, but for reasons that are still unclear Kelley refused. Burghley then asked for a supply of

Kelley's magic powder, calling upon his patriotism and sense of loyalty to Elizabeth in her time of need. Kelley never sent his powder and never returned to England; he was imprisoned by the the Emperor in the 1590s and died in 1597, apparently attempting to escape. This story shows that Elizabeth and Cecil took very seriously the idea of an alchemist having discovered the secret of the transmutation of metals. Far from it seeming the foolish practice of a conjurer or charlatan, the existence of the powder was viewed as an important proposition and occasioned considerable diplomatic activity as efforts were made to obtain some of it.

Elizabeth badly needed money in the latter part of her reign. She has often been accused of being mean, of being unduly parsimonious and having a keen eye for the acquisition of gifts and property. One of her first actions on coming to power was to reform the currency, and this took precedence even over religious reform. Without reform of the currency she would not have been able to raise an army and supply it, and since England was in a state of war military provision was essential. Towards the end of her reign the economic situation was again dire. Carrolly Erickson paints a depressing picture of the state of the realm:

> The 'grasping days' of the 1590s clutched at the elegantly ruffed throats of the courtiers and turned their customary greed and acquisitiveness to clawing theft. With trade withered by the war, monopolies were the only route to solvency, and the men in power battled one another for the right to control the sale of soap and leather and wine and starch. That the sale of monopolies led to disastrous inflation for the people at large and to court corruption on a massive scale did not make the system any less appealing to those caught up in it, for if they blamed anything or anyone for the twilight madness of the late Elizabethan economy, they blamed the Queen.[12]

Elizabeth came to the throne with the country in a state of economic crisis and died with it in the grip of another. In the years between, she had borrowed money heavily from overseas, attempted to enrich her coffers with stolen treasure brought back by her sea-captains from their piratical voyages, allowed many of the castles she had inherited to fall into ruins because she was unwilling to spend money on restoring them and finally sold some of her own precious collection of jewellery that she had spent so many years acquiring. Whether she was mean or simply cautious remains a question of opinion; but what became clear in the years during which she presided over the court was the unprecedented degree of corruption around her.

Throughout the reigns of the various Tudor monarchs there was a struggle among the new aristocracy for more and more power and property. The Reformation changed the map of English land-ownership, with the dissolution of the monasteries and subsequent reallocation of religious lands and then with the gradual dispossession of many of the old Catholic families. Moreover, the Tudors with their fragile power base created new generations of landed aristocracy, men from middle- or lower-class backgrounds who rose up the ladder through cunning or intellect and received gifts of land and titles as a reward for their services. In this respect the reign of Elizabeth is the culmination of a century of speculation and social aspiration, with the new rich out to become even richer. Elizabeth may have allowed her castles and manors to crumble and decay; her courtiers had other ideas. Leicester, Christopher Hatton, Cecil, to name but three, all built magnificent palaces, employing the finest architectural skills available, and Cecil rather coyly excused his huge residence of Theobalds in Hertfordshire by pointing out that he would not have extended it so much had Elizabeth not been so fond of visiting him there. The wheel of fortune turned to the advantage of many enterprising young *arrivistes* in the capitalistic hot-house of Elizabeth's court. As the Faerie Queen grew older and was no longer desired for her sexual attractiveness, courtiers flocked around her in search of more material favours.

Notes

1. Sir John Hayward, *Annals of the First Four Years of the Reign of Queen Elizabeth* (London: Camden Society, 1840), p. 17.
2. Wallace MacCaffrey, *The Shaping of the Elizabethan Regime* (London: Jonathan Cape, 1969).

3. John Neale, *Queen Elizabeth I* (Harmondsworth: Pelican, 1960), p. 69.
4. Frederick Chamberlin, *The Sayings of Queen Elizabeth* (London: John Lane, Bodley Head, 1923), pp. 138–43.
5. Castiglione's *Il Cortegiano* was translated as *The Book of the Courtier* by Cecil's brother-in-law Sir Thomas Hoby.
6. Poems quoted are taken from Leicester Bradner (ed.) *The Poems of Queen Elizabeth I* (Providence, Rhode Island: Brown University Press, 1964).
7. Quoted in Paul Johnson, *Elizabeth I: A Study in Power and Intellect* (London: Weidenfeld & Nicolson, 1974), p. 198.
8. Ibid., p. 432.
9. Andrew Gurr, *The Shakespearean Stage, 1574–1642* (Cambridge: Cambridge University Press, 1970), p. 21.
10. See Frances Yates, *The Rosicrucian Enlightenment* (London: Routledge & Kegan Paul, 1972).
11. Johnson, *Elizabeth*, p. 223.
12. Carolly Erickson, *The First Elizabeth* (London: Macmillan, 1983), p. 394.

4 'Dread Sovereigne Goddesse'

Some time in the years 1569–70 Elizabeth wrote her poem 'The Doubt of Future Foes' (mentioned in the previous chapter). It is a well-crafted piece, opening with a note of uncertainty — 'The doubt of future foes exiles my present joy' — and ending in a much more decisive tone:

Our realm brooks not seditious sects, let them elsewhere resort.
My rusty sword through rest shall first his edge employ.
To poll their tops that seek such change or gape for future joy.

There is a dark warning in these lines, for Elizabeth wrote them in the aftermath of the first serious attempt at rebellion against her, the Northern Rising of 1569. The Earls of Westmorland and Northumberland united with the Duke of Norfolk in a plot to overthrow Elizabeth. They planned to replace her with the Catholic Mary Queen of Scots, who had crossed the border into England early in the same year to seek Elizabeth's protection but had become Elizabeth's prisoner. The rising was effectively suppressed but was followed shortly afterwards by a second attempt at organised revolt, the Ridolfi Plot.

Roberto Ridolfi, a Florentine banker based in London, collaborated in a complex network of dissenting voices, including both Mary Queen of Scots and her would-be husband, the Duke of Norfolk, in an attempt to bring together enemies abroad and the opposition at home. This combination of forces, it was believed, would be sufficient to overthrow Elizabeth and replace her with Mary. It was a bold strategy which, although it was unmasked and the principal plotters executed, had serious repercussions.

Firstly, the combination of the Northern Rising and the Ridolfi Plot presented a threat that had to be taken seriously, though it is interesting to note that Elizabeth was reluctant to accept this. The Duke of Norfolk was arrested and committed for trial, but Elizabeth held back from signing his death warrant. In this she was acting against the general will of the Commons, where a motion was put asking for the Queen of Scots to be brought to trial as well. Mary was described as 'the most notorious whore in all the world', 'the monstrous and huge dragon and mass of the earth', and even in Elizabeth's own words as 'the daughter of dissent'. Her bishops informed Elizabeth that Mary had 'heaped up together all the sins of the licentious sons of David — adulteries, murders, conspiracies, treasons, and blasphemies against God'.

Feeling ran high against Mary and the plotters, and the anti-Catholic mood of the Commons was further reinforced by the issue in February 1570 of a papal bull, *Regnans in Excelsis*, which excommunicated Elizabeth, declared her a heretic and absolved her subjects from allegiance to her in the eyes of the Church of Rome. Having steered a careful line of moderation with regard to other European states Elizabeth was now compelled to take note of the extent of her enemies abroad. She had begun her reign with the problem of Scotland a thorn in her side, and after the Northern Rising and the Ridolfi Plot the Scottish question again became acute. She could neither ignore Scotland nor, after the Ridolfi Plot, could she afford to drop her vigilance with regard to other European nations. She had come to the throne surrounded by enemies, and the number of those enemies had increased rather than decreased; effective policing was necessary and careful diplomacy aided by good spying networks and capital were needed to ensure that England had a functional defence system. All these factors inevitably coloured economic policy at home.

Furthermore Elizabeth's reluctance to act against the Duke of Norfolk, let alone against the Queen of Scots, brought her into conflict with her own Parliament. Sir John Neale has documented the relationship between Elizabeth and her Parliaments in his two-volume study[1] and, although not all historians would agree with him, he makes the interesting point that the tendency in the Commons was towards an increasing radicalism, while Elizabeth herself remained a moderate and a traditionalist. This interpretation makes a great deal of sense, and is certainly more acceptable than the view which presents the clashes between Elizabeth and her Parliament as a conflict between a feminine and a masculine world-view. Elizabeth did have strong views about the virtues of tradition, and although she had no dynastic interests, she nevertheless saw herself as an upholder of certain important tenets. In clashes with the Commons she did not always win. In 1572 she signed Norfolk's death warrant and his subsequent execution appeased the hawks in her court. Looking back now with the advantage of centuries of hindsight, it is quite clear that the opinions expressed to Elizabeth by her Parliament, that the Queen of Scots was a source of danger to her so long as she remained alive and that Norfolk had to die as an example to other potential traitors, was an opinion based on sound common sense.

The year 1570 is a watershed in Elizabeth's reign, and marked the end of one stage of government. Elizabeth's unwillingness to be drawn into open conflict began to take second place to the needs of the time. MacCaffrey suggests that by 1572 'the Elizabethan regime had at last attained its majority'[2] and certainly it must have been obvious by then that there were not going to be any easy solutions. Elizabeth continued to play with the idea of a French marriage for several more years, but in 1570 she was thirty-seven and the prospect of her producing an heir was receding annually. The Commons were unhappy about the possibility of a Scottish succession, and when Parliament met in April 1571 a bill was passed barring Mary and her son from the English succession. Elizabeth took exception to this, which she saw as interference in the laws of succession, and demanded that it be redrafted. But the problem of Mary remained, and Elizabeth's tactics of non-confrontation became less and less feasible. In June 1571 she wrote a long letter to Sir Francis Walsingham, her ambassador in France who was negotiating for the marriage with the Duke of Anjou. In this letter she gives a detailed explanation of why she had ordered the imprisonment of one of her bishops, the Bishop of Ross:

> the evil parts done by the Bishop of Ross are such, and so dangerous to us and our State, as no Prince could suffer, as we think, the like, without some sharp revenge. For wherein the late rebellion in the North, we understood that he had given the heads of that rebellion confort to enter into the same, which he could not deny, being charged therewith . . . we were content to pass over the same, with hope that he would attend his causes only to the place he held, to be as an agent or minister for her, and not to intermeddle as he had done with our affairs and to trouble our State.[3]

There is almost a note of bewilderment, as Elizabeth goes on to relate how the Bishop had been secretly plotting 'with some of our nobility', and furthermore had been involved with rebels in the Low Countries. It is almost as though she refused to accept that machinations were constantly in operation against her, believing that if she demonstrated tolerance, she would receive the same in return. For someone so shrewd and so politically able this line of thought reveals an idealism that is surprising. In the age of Machiavelli, Elizabeth still seems to have believed in moderation and tolerance in matters of State, Church and personal relations.

Further evidence of Elizabeth's reluctance to commit the country to anything that she felt might be dangerous or damaging can be found in the long-drawn-out saga of the Low Countries. The English involvement in the struggles of the Low Countries against Spain has sometimes been presented in emotional terms; small Protestant states, oppressed by the might of the Catholic Spanish Empire, stage a series of revolts and appeal desperately to sympathetic England for help. Another, equally emotional view, accuses Elizabeth of prevarication and hyprocrisy when she failed to send the kind of military aid that the Flemish rebels wanted. Certainly the question of English involvement in the Low Countries was an emotional issue at the time, and with some 30,000 refugees in England by 1560 people were constantly reminded of the problem. But far more crucial to Elizabeth's thinking was the blunt question of the economic consequences of English involvement. More than three-quarters of all English exports were woolen cloth, and this trade passed through Antwerp and the Low Countries. The question of finding alternative trading centres in Northern Europe occupied a good deal of energy in the 1560s, and eventually an agreement was made with Hamburg — only just in time, for in 1567 the Duke of Alba entered the Low Countries with 10,000 troops to quell the revolt. The following year all English merchants in the Low Countries were arrested and trade came to a sudden halt. That this crisis also happened at the same time as the Northern Rising only increased tension. Elizabeth ordered retaliation against the subjects of Philip II working in England, and relations between Spain and England took a sharp downward turn. Antwerp remained closed for five years, with serious consequences for the English trade and economy, and relations with Spain continued to deteriorate until the eventual open conflict of 1588.

Elizabeth's policy regarding the Low Countries was therefore a complex tangle of threads. There were important economic considerations, for the wool trade was at the heart of English stability, and there were equally important political issues. The traditional enemy of England had always been France, not Spain, and although anti-Spanish feeling had run high since the reign of Mary, Elizabeth continued to see France as the greatest threat. She must have wanted to see the Spanish army out of the Netherlands, particularly as stories of atrocities filtered across the Channel, but she was also concerned that France should not have a foothold in the Low Countries either. Moreover, although William of Orange, leader of the resistance movement, was a Protestant, he was a Calvinist and Elizabeth had little sympathy for extreme Protestantism. She wrote aggressively to William in 1579 complaining about Flemish treatment of English merchants and earlier in 1577, when Don John of Austria was recognised as leader of the Netherlands, she sent him a message of congratulation. Elizabeth wanted peace rather than war in the Low Countries, she saw the continuation of a Spanish presence as a safeguard against the French and was aware of the need to re-establish trade links with Antwerp.

In December 1577 Cecil sent a long memorandum to the Queen, pointing out the dangers of her pro-Spanish stance and arguing that Spain would not be long in striking directly against England. He acknowledged Elizabeth's reluctance to become directly involved in the Low Countries, recognising her unwillingness to shed English blood in support of foreign causes, her fears of antagonising her Catholic neighbours and her antipathy towards supporting rebels against their lawful sovereign. As Elizabeth played with the prospect of marriage to Alençon and Alençon played with the idea of becoming the saviour of the Low Countries himself, Cecil stayed mindful of the potential crisis with Spain. In 1584 that crisis came.

In June 1584 Alençon died and in July William of Orange was assassinated. Elizabeth's choices were severely limited; she could intervene in the Low Countries with French assistance, or she could act alone; either way she would alienate Spain. Eventually, in 1585, when Spain seized English ships and she could prevaricate no longer, she sent an army of some 7,000 men into the Low

Countries, led by the ageing Earl of Leicester. Elizabeth issued a statement to the effect that she saw herself as fighting a 'defensive' war, but essentially she had been forced to take a public stand.

The Leicester expedition ran into problems immediately. The Dutch had previously offered the sovereignty of the Netherlands to Elizabeth; now they offered Leicester the Governor-Generalship and he accepted. His progress through the Netherlands was that of a triumphal prince, with lavish celebrations and public feasting. Leicester's wife prepared to join him, assembling great quantities of household trappings fitting to the consort of a quasi-monarch. Elizabeth's rage at hearing of this was terrible. She wrote to Leicester, accusing him of betraying her trust and demanding that he obey her orders (see above, p. 42–3) and she sent Sir Thomas Heneage to Leicester to bring him back into line:

> You shall let the Earl understand how highly upon just cause we are offended with his late acceptation of the government of those provinces, being done contrary to our commandment delivered unto him both by ourself in speech and by particular letters from certain of our Council written unto him in that behalf by our expresse direction, which we do repute to be a very great and strange contempt, least looked for at his hands, being he is a creature of our own. . . .[4]

The campaign in the Low Countries went from bad to worse. The death of Sir Philip Sidney sent the nation into mourning, though Elizabeth herself did not attend the state funeral that was held in honour of him. She had difficulty in raising the money to pay her troops, the army was riddled with corruption (Shakespeare's satire on captains was firmly based on reality) and the war effort was becoming unpopular. Never liked at the best of times in the country at large, Leicester was attacked for mismanagement and financial irresponsibility. English involvement in the Low Countries was not a success.

In the spring of 1587 Walsingham, head of Elizabeth's competent spy network, gave her a paper entitled 'A plot for Intelligence out of Spain', which offered details of improving that network. Certainly it seems to have been effective, for Elizabeth was kept constantly informed of the preparations for the Spanish invasion of England, as Philip assembled his mighty Armada in

1587. The prospect of invasion changed the situation in England again, and Elizabeth was forced to take defensive measures and establish a strategy for dealing with the arrival of the Spanish fleet and the eventual landing of a Spanish army.

Philip II had probably decided to attack England as early as 1585, using the dangerous heresy of Elizabeth as an excuse to win sympathy with the Pope. He encountered one setback in 1587, when Drake sailed into Cadiz and attacked some Spanish ships while still in port (the famous 'singeing of the King of Spain's beard') but the Armada did not finally sail until July 1588. The destruction of the great Spanish fleet, the appalling loss of life (two-thirds of the crews died) has long been seen as one of the great English victories, with the image of a tiny beleaguered nation taking on the might of a major power and winning with the help of tactical naval skill, the geographical configuration of the British Isles, and the elements. Paintings, ballads and performers celebrated the 'Protestant wind' which had blown the Spanish fleet to destruction.

Elizabeth remained in London for the first stages of the conflict, so the popular image of her standing beside Drake on Plymouth Hoe staring out to sea is a piece of romantic fiction. When the Armada had effectively been driven away from English shores and the threat of invasion receded, Elizabeth went down to Tilbury and addressed her troops in one of the most famous speeches of her reign. Dressed in white, carrying a small silver truncheon in her hand and with her orange wig uncovered, she made a powerfully emotional address:

> I have always believed myself that, under God, I have placed my chiefest strength and safeguard in the loyal hearts and good will of my subjects; and therefore am come amongst you, as you see, at this time, not for my recreation and disport, but being resolved, in the midst and heat of the battle, to live or die amongst you all, and to lay down for God, for my kingdom and for my people, my honour and my blood, even in the dust.

She was well aware of the problems of a state at war being ruled by a woman, and perhaps wanted to take on that possible criticism in the next part of her speech: 'I know I have the body of a weak and feeble woman, but I have the heart and stomach of a king, and of a king of England too'.

While not recognising any inferiority in herself on account of her sex, Elizabeth often paid lip-service to the prejudices about women that circulated in her realm, not least of which was the belief in woman's inherent weakness. It was a useful oratorical device and an effective way of silencing critical voices. The Armada speech was by no means the first or last time she used it.

The defeat of the Armada did not solve many problems other than the immediate threat of invasion. The involvement in the Low Countries had been costly, many of Elizabeth's principal advisers were growing old and ill, Elizabeth herself was fifty-five and her policies of appeasement had been outpaced by time. She had forgiven Leicester for his presumption in the Netherlands campaign, and had appointed him commander of the Tilbury camp, but in August 1588 he broke up the camp and travelled to Buxton to take the waters, probably suffering from stomach cancer. He died in early September, and whatever pleasure Elizabeth may have derived from the celebrations of the greatest English victory since the battle of Agincourt was coloured by the enormity of her personal loss. Three years later in 1591, Christopher Hatton, her other long-standing favourite, also died. At the very point in her life when the threat of invasion and deposition could finally be set aside, Elizabeth lost the men who perhaps had come to symbolise her youth.

There was another side to the relationship Elizabeth shared with Leicester and Hatton. Romantic biographers have made much of the personal feelings present on both sides, but it is also the case that both men used their positions of power to amass wealth — often by unscrupulous means. Elizabeth granted both of them privileges she withheld from others, though she was also cognisant of her own generosity. After Leicester's death she secured his property against debts to the Crown, seizing back Kenilworth Castle and his lands in Warwickshire. The cost of maintaining appearances at court was high, and borrowing from the Crown one way of easing the burden.

The burden weighed far more heavily on the shoulders of the common people, particularly in rural areas. During Elizabeth's reign large areas of land were enclosed, to increase production of wool in some places and also for the benefit of the new land-hungry classes. Philip Stubbs in 1583 claimed that: 'These inclos-

ures be the causes why rich men eat up poor men as beasts do
eat grass. . . . They take in and inclose commons, moors, heaths,
and other common pastures, whereout the poor commonalty
were wont to have all their forage and feeding for their cattle, and
(which is more) corn for themselves to live upon'.[5] Enclosing the
land created hardship among the poor, all the more so when
contrasted with the great wealth enjoyed by the new rich, though
opinion is divided as to the extent of the unrest. Johnson, for
example, claims that Elizabeth's reign was 'singularly free of
rural disorder provoked by food shortages',[6] though Black claims
that the 'most striking feature of rural history between 1558 and
1603 was the prevalence of unrest', and goes on to say that this
unrest was caused principally by enclosure of land.[7] What is clear
is that poor harvests in the late 1580s combined with a rapid rise
in food prices to exacerbate the enclosure problem, and the
number of paupers and vagrants mushroomed. Paul Slack cites
the Bridewell records in London for the punishing of vagrants; in
1560–1 there were 69 vagrants punished, but by 1578–9 that
number had risen to 209 and by 1600–1 the number was 555.
Legislation passed in 1572 (the year that also absolved actors
from the category of vagrants) tightened up on the treatment of
the homeless poor. Pauper children were to be bound out to
service, vagrants were to be whipped and bored through the
gristle of the right ear.[8] Other legislation laid down small sums
for local poor relief, and in some places houses of correction were
established. The category of those classified as vagrants covered a
large number of people, including wandering scholars, palmists,
fencers, players of interludes and minstrels who were not part of
any established company under the patronage of a nobleman,
pedlars, tinkers and anyone judged to be unwilling to work. Quite
how many wretched people roamed the countryside, having been
dispossessed of their meagre corner of land or been unable to find
employment and a roof in the expanding towns, remains unclear.
What is also unknown is how far these people contributed to the
mood of the country, whether they were hidden like the poor in
Britain and the United States in the 1980s or whether they were a
constant reminder of the other face of capitalism, as in contemporary Africa or Latin America. It seems likely, however, that the
seeds for the English Revolution which came not very long after
Elizabeth's passing were already laid in the latter years of her

reign, in the conflict between the harsh treatment of the ever-more-numerous poor and the extravagant displays of wealth by the new rich. Some of the clashes between Crown and Parliament involved aspects related to these issues, most notably in the November session of 1601.

Demands from the Commons for Elizabeth to revoke some of the large number of monopoly patents she had granted had become so strong that they could no longer be ignored. Persuaded by Robert Cecil to act in order to calm the situation, Elizabeth made one of her forceful speeches. She began by saying that her principal jewel was the love for her people — 'For I do esteem it more than any treasure or riches' — and that her sole desire was to see their prosperity: 'Of myself I must say this: I never was any greedy, scraping grasper, nor a strait fast-holding Prince, nor yet a waster. My heart was never set on any wordly goods, but only for my subjects' good. What you bestow on me, I will not hoard it up, but receive it to bestow on you again. . . '.

At this juncture in her speech, she invited the Commons to rise from their knees and went on to justify her policy on monopolies: 'Since I was Queen, yet did I never put my pen to any grant but that, upon pretext and semblance made unto me, it was both good and beneficial to the subject in general, though a private profit to some of my ancient servants who had deserved well at my hands'. Nevertheless, she said, if her giving of grants were the cause of abuse and oppression she would see to it that the offenders were punished:

> If my kingly bounties have been abused, and my grants turned to the hurt of my people, contrary to my will and meaning, and if any in authority under me have neglected or perverted what I have committed to them, I hope God will not lay their culps and offences to my charge; who, though there were danger in repealing our grants, yet what danger would I not rather incur for your good, than I would suffer them still to continue?[9]

She acknowledged the role she played in the well-being of the country, but reminded her listeners that there were two sides to the coin:

> To be a King and wear a crown is a thing more glorious to them that see it, than it is pleasant to them that bear it. For

myself, I was never so much enticed with the glorious name of a King or royal authority of a Queen, as delighted that God hath made me His instrument to maintain His truth and glory, and to defend this Kingdom (as I said) from peril, dishonour, and tyranny and oppression.

Finally, she returned to the question of her sex:

Shall I ascribe anything to myself and my sexly weakness? I were not worthy to live then; and, of all, most unworthy of the mercies I have had from God, who hath given me a heart that yet never feared any foreign or home enemy. And I speak it to give God the praise, as a testimony before you, and not to attribute anything to myself. For I, oh Lord, what am I, whom practises and perils past should not fear? Or what can I do? That I should speak for any glory, God forbid.

It is recorded that she spoke these last words 'with a great emphasis'. This speech, which she liked sufficiently to have printed and circulated by the royal printer, has become known as Elizabeth's 'Golden Speech'. It gives some idea of her skills in public speaking, her bluntness and her defensiveness, along with her sense of her own place in the hierarchy and her belief in her divine mission. The armies of the dispossessed, the crafty acquisitive courtiers and the new-rich middle classes can hardly have accorded with her desires for the well-being of her people and it is understandable that many biographers have sought to exonerate her from responsibility for such events. Others, however, have apportioned a good deal of blame to her, suggesting that her style of government and her continued vacillation led inevitably to a great deal of power passing into the hands of those around her. There is evidence that things were often kept hidden from her, and that decisions were frequently taken for her, without her knowledge, particularly as she grew older and the machinery of government became more cumbersome.

Elizabeth's greatest interest in terms of government seems to have been in the wheeling and dealing of international diplomacy rather than in carving out new domestic legislation. Her ecclesiastical policies, which will be discussed in the next chapter, took up a great deal of time and energy, particularly in the first half of her reign, and were among her greatest successes, but it was overseas affairs that fascinated her and to which she gave considerable attention.

During Elizabeth's reign, English naval power increased steadily and the basis for the British Empire was firmly laid. In 1562 John Hawkins, later to be knighted and appointed Treasurer of the Navy in 1578, sailed to West Africa, bought a cargo of black slaves and then sailed across the Atlantic to Hispaniola, where he sold them for gold, silver and sugar. Three years later in 1565 he set off on another voyage, and this time Elizabeth invested in the enterprise and contributed one of her own ships. The Spanish ambassador protested that English merchants were not entitled to trade on Spanish colonial soil; the Spaniards held the monopoly of the slave trade to the West Indies and the importation of goods back to Europe, but Elizabeth continued to turn a blind eye to the activities of her maritime entrepreneurs, and at the same time continued to accept whatever they brought back. Clearly New World trading was a good investment, and for a queen who was short of money it represented a tempting solution to financial problems. In 1581, Francis Drake circumnavigated the globe and returned with the contents of a Spanish treasure ship. The shareholders entitled to some of the profits included Elizabeth, Leicester, Walsingham and Hatton. The Spanish ambassador protested at Elizabeth's apparent open acceptance of Drake's piratical activities, but the money continued to flood in. With the difficulties experienced by the closure of the port of Antwerp, it was only logical that there would be considerable investment in other overseas trading ventures.

Romantic biographers and film-makers have made much of the relationship between Elizabeth and Drake. He has been depicted as a charismatic figure, a lovable rogue, a champion of English Protestantism against the villainous Spaniards. He was certainly an extraordinary man, combining great navigational skills with considerable courage and daring, and was also a very cultivated one. During his expedition of 1589 he took with him some boy singers loaned from the city of Norwich, since he enjoyed listening to music while dining. But behind the adventuring and the delicate manners, there was a man bent on making hard profits. The slave trade between Africa and the New World was a source of solid income; it was developed unscrupulously and calculatedly and the cargoes of desperate human beings that crossed the ocean one way were ruthlessly traded for goods that could be sold back in England and make the carrier a wealthy man.

The contrasts of the age of Elizabeth are particularly striking today. On the one hand there was an intense concern with religion, strong moral values and the growth of a democratic parliamentary structure that was considerably more enlightened than many of the systems in operation elsewhere in Europe, where absolutism prevailed for centuries to follow. But on the other hand there were the armies of vagrants, the new poor crushed beneath the rising classes, the shiploads of slaves destined for misery and death across the ocean. The greatness of Elizabethan England, its architectural marvels, its wealth of culture, its beauty and its splendour concealed the darkness of starvation, slavery and death by frequent attacks of plague.

The war of nerves against Spain, with English privateers attacking the Spanish treasure fleets and trying to break into new markets in the Caribbean and the Pacific, continued for many years . The declaration of war between the two countries and the defeat of the Armada in 1588 did not radically change this state of affairs, and Elizabeth was criticised for not following up the defeat of the Armada with full-scale destruction of Spanish sea power. Sir Walter Raleigh later stated bluntly that Elizabeth was to blame for the failure to destroy the Spanish overseas empire:

> If the late Queen would have believed her men of war as she did her scribes, we had in her time beaten that great empire in pieces and made their kings kings of figs and oranges as in old times. But her Majesty did all by halves and by petty invasions taught the Spaniard how to defend himself, and to see her own weakness which, till our attempts taught him, was hardly known to himself.[10]

Elizabeth was not a war-monger, and she used her naval and military power to hold a position of balance rather than to act aggressively. It is interesting to note the terms of Raleigh's accusation; she did not listen so well to her men of war as she did to her scribes, and did all by halves. It is a criticism that I find reassuring; in an age of violence and profiteering, Elizabeth held to her principles. She may have been Machiavellian in her dealings with people, but she was not an aggressor though, ironically, it was her non-aggression and desire for appeasement that opened the way for profiteers to abuse the system.

Notes

1. John Neale, *Elizabeth I and her Parliaments*, vol. I, *1559–81*, vol. II, *1584–1601* (London: Jonathan Cape, 1949–57).
2. W. MacCaffrey, *The Shaping of the Elizabethan Regime* (London: Jonathan Cape, 1969), p. 316.
3. Letter to Sir Francis Walsingham, 8 June 1571, repr. in G. B. Harrison, *The Letters of Queen Elizabeth* (London: Cassell, 1935), pp. 97–100.
4. Letter to Sir Thomas Heneage, 10 February 1586, repr. ibid., pp. 170–4.
5. Philip Stubbs, quoted in J. B. Black, *The Reign of Elizabeth, 1558–1603* (Oxford: Clarendon Press, 1959), p. 252.
6. Paul Johnson, *Elizabeth: A Study in Power and Intellect* (London: Weidenfeld & Nicolson, 1974), p. 212.
7. J. B. Black, *The Reign of Elizabeth 1558–1603* (Oxford: The Clarendon Press, 1936), p. 252.
8. Paul Slack, 'Poverty and Social Regulation in Elizabethan England', in Christopher Haigh (ed.), *The Reign of Elizabeth I* (London: Macmillan, 1984), pp. 221–41.
9. Elizabeth's speech is quoted in full in Neale, *Elizabeth I and her Parliaments*, II, pp. 388–91.
10. E. Edwards, *Life and Letters of Sir Walter Raleigh*, vol. I.

1. Elizabeth as a Young Girl. Artist unknown, c. 1542–7. Elizabeth's tutor Roger Ascham said that 'so much solidity of understanding, such courtesy united with dignity, have never been observed at so early an age'. This portrait gives the image of a serious and learned young woman. *(See pp. 22–3, 125–6.)*

2. The Coronation Portrait. Artist unknown, c. 1559. Elizabeth in
her coronation robes holds the orb and sceptre. She wears her
hair loose as a sign of virginity, and gazes straight out at the
onlooker. This highly stylised portrait gives an image of a woman
firmly set on the path to greatness. *(See pp. 52–3, 126.)*

3. Chalk drawing of Elizabeth by Federigo Zuccaro, 1575. This drawing of Elizabeth, companion to one of Robert Dudley, is unique in having been drawn in the Queen's presence. Behind her the pillar represents Constancy, the serpent Prudence, the dog Fidelity, and the ermine Chastity. *(See p. 14.)*

4. The Ditchley Portrait. Artist unknown, c. 1592. The ageing
Elizabeth, lavishly dressed and bejewelled despite the sunken
features and tense expression, stands (her feet oddly out of line
with her body) on Ditchley in Oxfordshire where she went in
September 1592 for a ceremonial visit. The symbolism here
reflects the growing cult of Elizabeth the Great. *(See pp. 125–6.)*

5. Marble head on Elizabeth's tomb in Westminster Abbey.
Sculpted by Maximilian Colte, coloured and gilded by Nicholas
Hilliard and John de Critz.
In death Elizabeth's sharp features appear much more weighty;
her mouth is set decisively and her eyes stare blankly into the
void. *(See pp. 126.)*

Genealogical Table

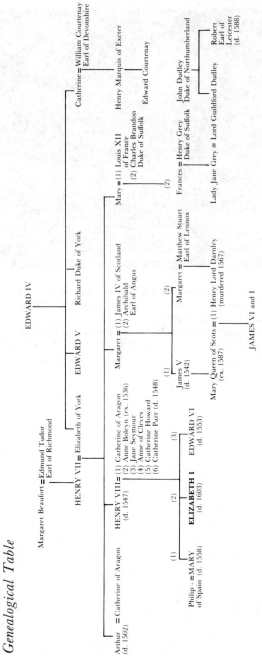

Margaret Beaufort = Edmund Tudor
Earl of Richmond

Catherine = William Courtenay
Earl of Devonshire

HENRY VII = Elizabeth of York

EDWARD IV

Richard Duke of York

EDWARD V

Henry Marquis of Exeter

Edward Courtenay

Arthur = Catherine of Aragon
(d. 1502)

HENRY VIII = (1) Catherine of Aragon
(d. 1547)   (2) Anne Boleyn (ex. 1536)
             (3) Jane Seymour
             (4) Anne of Cleves
             (5) Catherine Howard
             (6) Catherine Parr (d. 1548)

Margaret = (1) James IV of Scotland
           (2) Archibald
               Earl of Angus

Mary = (1) Louis XII
           of France
       (2) Charles Brandon
           Duke of Suffolk

(1)
Philip - = MARY (d. 1558)
of Spain

(2)
ELIZABETH I
(d. 1603)

(3)
EDWARD VI
(d. 1553)

(1)
James V
(d. 1542)

(2)
Margaret = Matthew Stuart
Earl of Lennox

(2)
Frances = Henry Grey
Duke of Suffolk

John Dudley
Duke of Northumberland

Mary Queen of Scots = (1) Henry Lord Darnley
(ex. 1587)   (murdered 1567)

Lady Jane Grey = Lord Guildford Dudley

Robert
Earl of
Leicester
(d. 1588)

JAMES VI and I

5 Defender of the (Heretic) Faith

During the years of Mary's reign Elizabeth had taken great care to tread a non-controversial line in matters of religion. On the one hand, she had endeavoured to placate Mary by paying lip-service at least to Catholic ceremonies, and on the other she had maintained her position in the eyes of the English public as the Protestant hope for the future. When she succeeded to the throne she maintained the same canny position of non-commitment for the first few weeks of her reign, while she picked a team of advisers whose first loyalty would be to her, whatever their religious preferences. Letters from the initial stages of her reign show the kind of confusion and doubt that her tactics caused, and once Parliament had been summoned in January 1559, and Elizabeth's middle-of-the-road position began to emerge more clearly, there was a sense of dissatisfaction both among supporters of the Catholic and Protestant causes. The Duke de Feria wrote to his master Philip II in March about the 'vile rabble' of heretics who were pouring across the Channel back into England and being 'greatly congratulated' upon their coming.[1] One day later the Protestant clergyman, later Bishop of Salisbury, John Jewel, wrote to Peter Martyr in Zurich that the Roman religion was only just beginning to be changed:

> The bishops are a great hindrance to us; for being, as you know, among the nobility and leading men in the Upper House, and having none there on our side to expose their artifices or confute their falsehoods, they reign as sole monarchs in the midst of ignorant and weak men, and easily overreach our little party, either by their numbers or their reputation for learning.

Nor did Jewel feel that Elizabeth was living up to expectations: 'The Queen, meanwhile, though she openly favours our cause, yet is wonderfully afraid of allowing any innovations: this is owing partly to her own friends, by whose advice everything is carried on, and partly to the influence of Count Feria, a Spaniard, and Philip's ambassador'.[2] In fact, far from being an influence on Elizabeth, de Feria quarrelled with her regularly, as his letters testify. On one occasion he had the temerity to point out to her that her idea of ruling as her father had done and restoring his religion was an absurd dream, noting also that Henry had burned Lutherans at the stake. De Feria's problems increased as Elizabeth seemed to swing further and further away from Rome, and then the rug was pulled from under his feet when Philip suddenly abandoned his negotiations for marriage with Elizabeth and announced his forthcoming marriage with Elizabeth de Valois, daughter of the King of France. Nevertheless it is significant that John Jewel could read the situation in such a way. Elizabeth had obviously very deliberately kept the issue clouded.

Jewel's point about the bishops was an important one. A first step had to be the replacement of the Marian bishops with a new team of Protestant supporters, even though, as has often been pointed out, the old Catholic Church leaders adopted a policy of passive resistance, not of active opposition. Throughout her reign Elizabeth found that she could rely on the loyalty of Catholic supporters to the Crown and to herself, despite the frequent fears of some of her advisers (and the hopes of some of her enemies) that Catholics would form an active group committed to her overthrow. Nevertheless, although she retained some Catholics in her government, the firm opposition of the Marian bishops to some of the changes proposed by Parliament led inevitably to their removal from office.

Paul Johnson argues that it is impossible to determine exactly what Elizabeth's beliefs were, but it is quite clear that she preferred a tolerant form of religion.[3] She seems to have been in favour of religious rites being performed in English and not in Latin, and to have rejected some of the more elaborate ceremonial, though she approved of the use of church vestments and was fond of religious music. Her attitude appears to have been that she would have preferred the establishment of a state religion as a formality, and then left it to the individual to worship with whichever rite he or she might choose. Once the Marian bishops made it clear that they were going to resist even moderate changes, however, the pressure grew for more radical changes that would definitively restrict their power. No doubt Elizabeth resented this deeply; the combined forces of the Catholic bishops and the Protestants in the Commons ensured that her ideals of tolerance could not be put into practice. In a letter dated 6 December 1559, her anger is clear enough as she attacks five of the bishops who had been deprived of their sees for refusing to accept the new order and had then written appealing to her to reject schisms and heresies and to return to the Church of Rome.

> As to your entreaty for us to listen to you, we waive it: yet do return you this answer. Our realm and subjects have been long wanderers, walking astray, whilst they were under the tuition of Romish pastors, who advised them to own a wolf for their head (in lieu of a careful shepherd), whose inventions, heresies and schisms be so numerous, that the flock of Christ have fed on poisonous shrubs for want of wholesome pasture.[4]

Warming to her theme, Elizabeth then went on to tell the bishops who, she claimed, had 'hit us and our subjects in the teeth' with their account of how the Church of Rome had brought Christianity to Britain, that they were liars and that their account was at variance with history. British Christianity, she argued, had developed along other lines:

> As for our father being withdrawn from the supremacy of Rome by schismatical and heretical counsels and advisors; who, we pray, advised him more, or flattered him, than you, good Mr Hethe, when you were bishop of Rochester? And than you, Mr Boner, when you were archdeacon? And you, Mr Turberville? Nay further, who was more an advisor of our father, than your great Stephen Gardiner, when he lived? Are not ye then those schismatics and heretics? If so, suspend your evil censures. Recollect, was it our sister's conscience made her so averse to our father's and brother's actions, as to undo what they had perfected? Or was it not you, or such like advisors, that dissuaded her, and stirred her up against us and other of the subjects?

This outraged letter ends on a note of warning; the bishops are told to refrain from making similar statements 'lest you provoke us to execute those penalties enacted for the punishing of our resisters'. The tone of this letter indicates how outraged Elizabeth must have been. Her father's breach with Rome had, after all, been linked to his marriage with her mother, and somewhere beneath the formal statements of religious position, she must have been aware of that fact and of the part played by advisers in her mother's subsequent disgrace and death.

In the Parliament of 1559 the great Elizabethan religious compromise was finally worked out, and the Act of Supremacy and the Act of Uniformity were passed. It seems clear that Elizabeth was forced to take up a more dogmatic position than she would have wished for, and that she was also forced to accept certain things that she found objectionable (the abolition of celibacy for clergy was a case in point). Elizabeth disliked married priests, but they had become firmly established in the reformed Churches and had obviously come to stay. The Act of Supremacy re-established the monarch as head of the Church, and all clergy were compelled to swear an oath of allegiance to the Queen. This was completely unacceptable to those members of the clergy whose loyalty was primarily to the Pope in religious matters, and their refusal to take the oath led to their removal from office.

Elizabeth had inherited a very difficult religious legacy from the other members of her family. Despite the popular mythology of subsequent centuries, which has seen Henry as a champion of English Protestantism, his form of reformed religion was very mild indeed. His assumption of the title of Supreme Head of the Church was as much a political gesture as a religious one, and he continued to hear Mass throughout his life. Edward VI, on the other hand, had been a far more extreme Protestant, firmly opposed to Roman Catholicism, and in his reign the Prayer Book was radically reformed, first in 1549 and again in 1552. The accession of Mary had worsened the situation in the country at large; despite her devotion and her good intentions the horrors of the mass burnings and tortures of those who refused to return to the Church of Rome had implanted the spectre of Catholic unreasonableness in the minds of the people. Foxe's *Book of Martyrs*, which appeared in 1563, became a best seller second only to the Bible, and a whole generation grew up reared on accounts of the vileness of Catholic persecutions. Moreover, horrific stories from the rest of Europe filtered through regularly; the King of Spain and his family attended mass burnings of heretics, known as *autos-da-fé*, accompanied by elaborate public ceremonial; the power of the Inquisition grew steadily as attention focused on combating the rise of heresy with the spread of the Reformation. All the signs indicated the emergence of a new force, the Counter-Reformation of the Catholic Church. In such a climate a policy of moderation and tolerance was a difficult one to argue for, and it is remarkable that Elizabeth was able to accomplish so much in this respect, even while conceding ground in other ways. Paul Johnson summarises her position succinctly:

> In all probability, she would have happily settled for the first Edwardian Prayer Book of 1549, virtually an English translation of the Mass — with the Consecration omitted. But this was not what happened. Indeed, in some ways, the religious settlement of 1559 was a defeat for the Queen; or, to put it another way, an important stage in her political education.[5]

The Act of Supremacy was a compromise in itself, because, as I mentioned in Chapter 2 (p. 38), Elizabeth shrewdly refused to accept the title of 'Supreme Head' and allayed the objections of Catholics and of Protestants opposed to a woman heading the Church, by taking instead the title 'Supreme Governor'. The Act of Uniformity resulted in the Book of Common Prayer of 1559, which closely followed the 1552 Prayer Book with slight modifications, rather than Elizabeth's own preference for the less radical Prayer Book of 1549. Church attendance was made compulsory, marriage for the clergy established as a principle and England firmly brought into the Protestant camp. Elizabeth's concessions were probably inevitable; unrest in the country at large had resulted in a series of attacks on churches, with the destruction of statues and relics, symbols of Roman Catholicism. Had Elizabeth delayed any longer, or refused to concede on more points, the scale of the unrest could have been much greater.

Edward Rishton, a Catholic priest banished by Elizabeth in 1581, and author of a history of the English Reformation, accuses Elizabeth of hypocrisy:

> The queen is in the habit of boasting before strangers and the foreign ambassadors that the clergy of her sect are held in honour, and are not mere starvelings like those of Geneva, and other Churches of the kind, not so well ordered as hers; and

that she had not gone so far from the faith of other princes and of her own ancestors as many think. The better to keep up this fraud, she retained for some years on the table, which she had set up in the place of the altar, in her chapel, two wax candles, which were never lighted, with a silver crucifix between them. And then in order to please the Catholics, and to impose the more easily upon foreigners, she used to say from time to time that she was forced, not by her own convictions, but by the clamours of her subjects, to make a change of religion, but that she had practised great moderation in making it.[6]

Although presented as an attack on Elizabeth, this seems a reasonable assessment of her position regarding religious observance. In the early years of her reign, at least, she kept well away from any overt statements of prejudice, except for her strong feelings about married clergy and her refusal to allow Bishop Bonner to kiss her hand when she first entered London as Queen since she held him responsible for the burnings of Protestants during Mary's reign.

Elizabeth's conservatism in matters of religion was shared by many. Research is gradually bringing to light the extent to which older observances remained intact in different parts of the country. Conservative clergy continued to maintain Catholic ritual in the services, and the Prayer Book's command that bread be used in the Communion service instead of wafers was often ignored. Christopher Haigh quotes a splendid example of a disobedient parish — Weaverham in Cheshire — that in 1578 was accused of having no Communion Book, Bible or Homilies, of keeping an altar in the old manner, of having no linen cloth and covering for the communion table and no chest for the poor and of not keeping the register. Moreover:

The people will not be stayed from ringing the bells on All Saints' Day. They frequent alehouses in service time. Great talking used in the church. No levying for the poor of the absents from the church. Morris dances and rushbearing used in the church. Jane, an old nun, is an evil woman and teacheth false doctrine. They refuse to communicate with the usual bread. None cometh to the communion three times a year. They refuse to bring in their youth to be catechised. Crosses are standing in the churchyard.[7]

The parishioners of Weaverham were clinging on to their old traditions in ways that indicate how tenacious was the preservation of tradition, despite new government ordinances. The wheels of change ground slowly, and Elizabeth refused to follow her sister's tactics in forcibly imposing religious alternatives on the population, at least in the early years of her reign.

The problem with maintaining a position of religious tolerance in the sixteenth century was that religion was inextricably bound up with politics. When she came to the throne in 1558 Elizabeth had a series of immediate problems to tackle including the poor economic state of the country and the dangerous possibility of escalation of war abroad, besides the question of religious settlement. Later, however, matters of religion increased in seriousness, and after 1569 when Mary Queen of Scots fled to England, ostensibly to ask for Elizabeth's help but in fact to plot against her, it became less and less easy to maintain a position of neutrality in religious affairs. The Northern Rising and the Ridolfi Plot, coupled with the Pope's excommunication of Elizabeth made the situation worse still. The loyalty of Catholic subjects became once again a controversial issue; in a crisis of duties, where would Catholic subjects place their support — with Elizabeth, the Queen but also heretical monarch, or with her opponent the Catholic Queen of Scots whose claim to the throne was held by the Pope to be more acceptable? In fact, Elizabeth's belief that she held the pre-eminence in her people's hearts was closer to the truth, but the war of nerves fought between the Catholic hierarchy and the English government resulted in increased tension all around. The brutal killing of French Huguenots in the St Bartholomew's Day Massacre in 1572 added fuel to anti-Catholic feeling, and Elizabeth found herself led further along the road towards public statements of anti-Catholic feeling, in short towards persecution of the Catholic minority.

Regnans in Excelsis, the papal bull of excommunication, which absolved Catholics of their duty to Elizabeth, appeared in February 1570. Two years earlier, in 1568, an English college or seminary had been set up in Douai in Flanders by William Allen, a Catholic refugee, later Cardinal Allen, to serve as a training ground for those young Englishmen deprived of their Catholic inheritance. Other colleges followed — Rome in 1579, Valladolid in 1589 and Seville in 1592. These colleges became centres for the training of missionary priests whose vocation was to return to England to restore the old faith. Books were smuggled into England, priests crossed the Channel in disguise and began their missionary activities, and these ventures were financed by the leading Catholic powers, particularly by Spain. The policies and politics of the Counter-Reformation began to enter English life, and Parliament demanded stronger legislation to combat this growing movement. Elizabeth fought back, resisting the imposition of stronger penalties on Catholics, contriving to have punishments reduced for such activities as hearing Mass or non-attendance at Church of England services, but in 1585 she gave way and allowed the passing of an act which ordered all Jesuits and priests out of England immediately, on pain of being accused of high treason. All students at seminaries who did not present themselves before an English court officer to take the oath of loyalty were declared traitors; and anyone found supporting the seminaries or sending their children to study in such places was to be punished with heavy fines and imprisonment. In 1593 further legislation established harsher penalties; with that act against popish recusants, those people who refused to attend the Protestant service were forbidden to travel beyond a five-mile radius and were therefore effectively under local arrest.

In his study of the Reformation of England Philip Hughes gives figures of Catholics executed during the reign of Elizabeth.[8] Between 1577 and 1603, some 183 were executed, of whom 123 were priests, one a friar and the remainder lay people, three of whom were women. All but four of the priests executed had been in some way linked to the seminaries, and most had trained there. Death for recusant priests was a bloody and savage affair; the condemned man was hanged from a gallows, cut down while still alive and disembowelled, before being cut into pieces. This procedure, known as hanging, drawing and quartering, was used in the famous execution of three priests, Edmund Campion, Alexander Bryant and Ralph Sherwin in December 1581. All men showed signs of torture on their bodies (Campion's fingernails had been torn out), but died declaring their loyalty as Englishmen to Elizabeth.

The death of Edmund Campion, which caught the public imagination in a peculiarly horrific manner and effectively gave the Catholic cause its first martyrs, had widespread repercussions. Elizabeth, formerly presented as an immoral woman and a heretic in the eyes of the Roman Church, now became personified as the symbol of intolerance and brutality. Lord Burghley's attempt to justify torture in times of political crisis did not help the situation,[9] and relations between Elizabeth and Catholics at home and abroad deteriorated steadily. The defeat of the Armada in 1588 convinced her once more of the fundamental loyalty of her Catholic subjects, but by then the anti-Catholic cause had gained too much ground and the case against Elizabeth as a persecuting tyrant had been too well-developed. William Allen's *A True, Sincere and Modest Defence of English Catholiques*, which appeared in 1584, repeated the view that Elizabeth was in the grip of evil advisers, but in a letter to the Cardinal of Como in 1582 he described her as 'our Herodias'.[10]

Until the execution of Mary Queen of Scots in 1587 there was always the spectre (or vision, depending on point of view) of an alternative Queen of England. With Mary dead, and her son, who was known to be an ardent Protestant, next in line to the English throne the Catholic cause become a rearguard action rather than a forward-moving attack. But despite the gradual diminishing of Catholic power in the country at large, anti-Catholic feeling increased and became linked to expressions of national sentiment. Since both Spain and France were Catholic countries anti-Catholicism also became a point of focus for anti-French and anti-Spanish feeling. (The process whereby Catholicism began to be regarded as a foreign import rather than a native product is curiously similar to the process under way in Britain in the 1980s which attempts to portray socialism as a foreign import, despite the lengthy history of home-grown workers' movements and organisations over the past two hundred years.) There was considerable political capital to be made among the rising bourgeoisie with the repression of Catholicism; there were properties to be had, positions of power in local and central government to be obtained and land to be taken. Since the traditional centres of strong Catholic belief lay in the more sparsely populated areas at some distance from London — Norfolk, the north of England, Scotland and Ireland, the dispossession of Catholic landowners inevitably released large areas of land for the up-and-coming Protestant replacements. Case-studies of individual families at this time often reveal a sordid story of rapid changes in religion, as opportunities were seized upon and the path to wealth and ennoblement made smoother by taking over the properties of dispossessed Catholic families.

We do not have any evidence of how Elizabeth regarded such practices, if indeed she realised that they were going on. Despite her numerous progresses around the country and her populist appeal to the masses, she lived in a court context, surrounded by the aristocracy and new bourgeoisie and protected by her inner circle of advisers who at times deliberately kept her in ignorance of matters in which they did not want her involvement. We know, however, that she carefully studied all trials that might affect state security, and Paul Johnson believes that this means that she must have authorised the execution of Catholic priests and must bear some of the responsibility for those deaths.[11] He quotes the Lord Keeper, in 1595, recording the close attention Elizabeth paid to the selection of judges and justices of the peace: 'her Majesty, therefore, like a good housewife looking unto all her household stuff, took the book in her own hands and in the sight of us, the Lord Treasurer and the Lord Keeper, went through and noted those justices she would have continued in commission, and whom she thought not meet, and willed us to consider the rest'.[12]

Elizabeth's religious tolerance was doomed to failure, just as many of the enlightened views of the age of Humanism collapsed and vanished in the harsher years of the late Reformation and Counter-Reformation. In his play, *Rabelais*, performed in 1968, Jean-Louis Barrault compares the enlightened attitudes of Humanist thought to the open-minded idealism of the 1960s and notes with regret the passing of both.[13] Elizabeth had received a wide-ranging Renaissance education, studying many languages and taking an interest in numerous disciplines, but hers was the last generation of women to be educated in this way, and the changed mood of the late sixteenth century resulted in all kinds of repression — religious intolerance, increased restrictions on women's position in society, and more rigid class structuring with greater social divisiveness. As has often been pointed out, the fate of the theatre in England serves as a metaphor for other wider changes; as the great popular playhouses of the 1580s and 1590s declined in status and importance, so the new theatres came to be purpose-built for a smaller, elite audience at court. The playhouse with its mob of groundlings and mass enthusiasms was replaced by the lavish, private aristocratic theatre, and the gap between monarch and public widened similarly. Elizabeth's contact with her people was not a practice James wished to continue; when eventually Charles I died on the block, partly as a result of his inability to comprehend the size of the gulf between the ruler and subjects, the process of separation begun in the last years of Elizabeth's reign was finally obvious to all.

Elizabeth's foreign policy, and increasingly her domestic policy, came to be inextricably linked to matters of religion. After 1588 the Spanish threat finally disappeared, but another major problem had arisen, also with a direct religious connection. Looming off the English and Welsh coast was Ireland, a problem that had bedevilled England rulers since their first ill-fated attempts to colonise the island. Tudor Ireland has been compared to a bankrupt estate, a property without a clear governing policy, a place of poverty, dissent and smouldering rage with no political or racial unity. Fundamentally Catholic, Ireland had been largely ignored by Elizabeth until the whole question of reform of the English Church came into being. Then the matter of Irish Catholicism could not be ignored; since England faced the forces of Catholic Europe alone it was important to have some sense of British unity. Elizabeth cultivated the Protestant King of Scots, as her letters show, and could not risk having a pro-Catholic territory such as Ireland within the complex of the British Isles. Hence the beginning of the policy of introducing a Protestant state Church into Catholic Ireland, a policy whose disastrous consequences are still being felt at the end of the twentieth century.

In 1567 Sir Henry Sidney, sent to Ireland on a tour of inspection, wrote: 'I never was in a more pleasant country, but never saw I a more waste or desolate land, filled with ruined churches and burned-out villages and the bones and skulls of dead subjects, who, partly by murder and partly by famine, have died in the fields'.[11] The poverty of the people and the primitive conditions in which they lived meant that the Irish were widely regarded as barbarians, beings only one stage removed from the animal. Sidney commented on their morals in terms that saw his sense of outrage:

Surely there was never people that lived in more misery than they do, nor as it would seem of worse minds, for matrimony among them is no more regarded in effect than conjunction between unreasonable beasts. Perjury, robbery and murder counted allowable. Finally, I cannot find that they make any conscience of sin, and I doubt whether they Christen the children or no; for neither find I a place where it should be done, nor any person able to instruct them in the rules of a Christian.[15]

The appalling conditions in Ireland, coupled with the system of feudal overlordship and the fact that major landowners were absent from their estates in England ensured that uprisings would not be infrequent. There were risings in the early 1560s, again in the period 1569–72, and in 1579–83. These were suppressed, not only by direct intervention from England but also through the assistance of opposing clan factions, for the clan system in Ireland meant that internal enmities were as strong as the hatred directed against the English. The factions and civil warfare that raged in Ireland ensured that there was no common organisation, no unified revolt against English occupation in the early years of Elizabeth's reign. But with attempts to introduce the reformed Church of England into Ireland, a country in which the impact of the Reformation had barely been felt at all, the Catholic Church became a rallying point for dissident groups. Missionary priests from the Continent arrived in Ireland and the torture of the Cardinal Archbishop of Dublin by his Protestant counterpart created strong feelings of anti-Protestant–anti-English reaction.

In 1595 Hugh O'Neill, who had been made Earl of Tyrone in 1585, took the forbidden revolutionary title of 'the O'Neill' and began to muster support for a large-scale uprising. He negotiated with Spain for money and supplies to help in his war effort and in 1597 led a successful attack on English forces marching to relieve the besieged fort at the Blackwater, the commanding point for control of Ulster's southern communications. The reaction to Tyrone's victory was instant and enormous; it served as a rallying point for anti-English feeling, boosted the morale of Irish rebels and seriously alarmed Elizabeth in London, who could now see the magnitude of the Irish crisis. In September 1598, she wrote furious letters to the Lord Justices and the rest of the Council of Ireland, criticising their delay in reacting to Tyrone's revolt and their incompetence and corruption:

> Only this we may not hide, that it doth not a little trouble us to find so hard effect of all things from thence, considering the notable supplies of men, treasure and victuals more plentifully sent than ever heretofore; wherein, although we do not deny but many things concur to make that State more difficult to be recovered than in former time, yet is there no person, be he never of so vulgar judgements, but doth plainly see the notorious errors in that Government.[16]

She went on to be more explicit and to denounce the corruption of the military captains who not only try to 'cover their frauds' but also desert and encourage others to do the same. The defeat at the Blackwater she describes as a 'foul error to our dishonour', adding that the story of incompetence and military inadequacy has been going on too long:

> Not only our armies have come back with loss, or doing nothing, but in their absence other parts of our Kingdom have been left to be spoiled and wasted by the rebels; and though the universality of the rebellion may be used as a reason of the mischief, yet it is almost a miracle that with the charges of an army of eight or nine thousand men, the principal rebels of Leinster and Wexford and other places, should not be mastered, though the capital rebels have not there been reduced, a matter cried out on by all that either write or come out of Ireland.

The Irish disaster went from bad to worse. In 1599 Elizabeth sent the inexperienced Earl of Essex to Ireland as Lord Deputy, but his failure, like that of his predecessors, only exacerbated the situation. The collapse of Essex's fortunes, his trial and execution, which will be discussed in the next chapter, can only have served to intensify Elizabeth's bitterness regarding the situation in Ireland as a whole. She felt strongly that before she died the problem of Ireland had to be solved, or rather, that the Tyrone rebellion had to be crushed. In fact she lived long enough to see it happen; in 1602 Charles Blount, Lord Mountjoy successfully carried out the mission in which Essex had failed. Tyrone surrendered and the revolt collapsed. Elizabeth wrote to Mountjoy congratulating him and agreed to accept the advice of her Council to grant Tyrone pardon from execution if he submitted to her terms. She was, apparently, reluctant to agree to a stay of execution, and in her letter to Mountjoy of 17 February 1603, she points out that in her opinion the 'heinous offences committed by Tyrone' have made him 'unworthy to live'. Nevertheless, she did agree and laid down the terms for Tyrone's surrender.

The settlement in Ireland has been hailed as Elizabeth's last great political triumph. The rebellion was firmly put down and Ireland was brought under English control with the power of the old clan system in ruins. But the Irish solution reflects many of the contradictions inherent in Elizabeth's vision of the world, a vision which came to be out of step with the changed ideology of another generation. She had resisted firm policies for Ireland for years, preferring simply to leave it as an unresolved problem that cost her little in terms of money and prestige. Then, with the wave of anti-Catholic feeling, the threat from Spain and the very real fear that Ireland might contribute to the Spanish Catholic menace, she was forced to become more repressive in her tactics. But the years of inadequate administration and local corruption meant that the government of Ireland was a disastrous public relations exercise. Tyrone's rebellion received strong support, not only because of religious feeling but also because the milking of Ireland by English profiteering landlords was such an obvious abuse. After the suppression of the Tyrone revolt the situation worsened. The hardship of the Irish peasants in their primitive conditions, noted by Sidney, intensified, as soldiers were billeted in Ireland to keep the peace and new waves of profiteers and carpet-baggers crossed the Irish Sea in search of quick money. Moreover, the revolt and the English reaction to it hardened the profound emotional allegiances of the Irish people. The Catholic Church acquired a power it had not enjoyed previously, and became associated with Irish national sentiment. Although in one sense a triumph, the suppression of the Tyrone rebellion marked the beginning of centuries of warfare and bitterness between Ireland and the government in London.

As she grew older Elizabeth's attitudes to religion seem to have hardened somewhat. When Henri IV the French Protestant King was converted to Catholicism and agreed to terms with Catholic rebels, Elizabeth wrote him a strongly worded letter:

> Alas, what griefs, what regret, what groanings I feel in my soul at the sound of such news . . . My God, is it possible that any earthly respect should efface that terror wherewith Divine fear threatens us? Can we reasonably expect a good issue from an act so iniquitous? . . . Yet I hope that sounder inspiration shall come to you . . . And where you promise me all friendship and faith, I confess that I have dearly merited it, and of that I shall not repent, provided that you will not change your father: otherwise I shall be to you but a bastard sister, or at least not of the same father. For I shall prefer always the natural to the adopted, as God best knows, who guides you to the right way of the best feeling.[17]

She signed herself, rather wittily in view of the circumstances: 'Your very assured sister, if it be after the old manner; with the new, I have nothing to do'. Her fears of Henri's conversion related more to her concern that he might join the anti-English forces in Europe than to any profound conviction that he had joined the forces of evil, but nevertheless the tone of the letter and Elizabeth's consistent disapproval of those who became converts to Catholicism show that she held firm to the rightness of her chosen religious path. The movement towards a reformed Church had begun and she supported it wholeheartedly. Opposition to that Church, from whichever direction, was not something she could accept lightly.

The steady increase in anti-Catholic feeling and legislation through Elizabeth's reign is well-documented, but there was another source of opposition to Elizabeth's midde-of-the-road tactics. She was particularly antagonistic to extreme Protestant reform movements, and throughout her reign her hostility towards those who felt she had not moved far enough in the cause of Protestantism is apparent.

One of the features of Calvinism, apart from its desire to root out some of the abuses perceived in the older religious orders, was belief in the right of the clergy to intervene and control the moral lives of parishioners. Elizabeth objected to what she regarded as a theocratic menace; the statute insisting that all English men and women had to attend church on Sundays was not one that she welcomed and was forced upon her by radical consent of Parliament. She detested sermons, and the sermon was of course a key feature of the reformed services. She is recorded as having interrupted sermons, sent messages to the pulpit to preachers to cut their sermons short and tried to restrict herself only to suffering sermons during Lent. Since she heard sermons from her closet that opened into the chapel, she could keep her lattice closed if she wished and to shut out the offending sound altogether. Addressing Parliament in 1585, she expressed her feelings about the increase in Puritan or episcopalian practices:

> You suffer many ministers to preach what they list and to minister the sacraments according to their own fancies, some one way, some another, to the breach of unity; yea, and some of them so curious in searching matters above their capacity as they preach they wot not what — that there is no Hell but a torment of conscience. Nay, I have heard there be six preachers in one diocese the which do six sundry ways. I wish such men to be brought into conformity and unity: that they minister the Sacraments according to the order of this Realm and preach all one truth; and that such as be found not worthy to preach, be compelled to read homilies . . . . for there is more learning in those than in twenty of some of their sermons. And we require you that you do not favour such men, being carried away with pity, hoping of their conformity, and inclining to noblemen's letters and gentlemen's letters, for they will be hanged before they be reformed.[18]

Elizabeth's struggle against radical reforms in the Church was another lost cause. As the older generation of bishops died out, the new ones came from a generation heavily influenced by the movement in Geneva and elsewhere in Protestant Europe. In 1577 there was a head-on clash between Elizabeth and her Archbishop of Canterbury Edmund Grindall over the issue of sermons and the licensing of preaching meetings. Grindall was suspended from office, but Elizabeth refused to allow him to resign and so the archbishopric of Canterbury remained on ice for six years until his death in 1583. She took care to ensure that his successor was a man who would act as a strong disciplinarian to bring the ragged lines of the newly formed Church into order, and appointed John Whitgift, the man she called her little black husband, another Calvinist but a man with a strong belief in hierarchical order. His task was to bring order to the new Church, to act against Catholic and Protestant extremists and to steer the middle way preferred by the Queen. Whitgift was a hard man, and it is significant that Elizabeth felt that she needed someone as narrow minded and intolerant as he to carry out her wishes.

A prime feature of Elizabeth's policy, in regard to matters of religion as in everything else, was a belief in the divine order of things. A monarch, once enthroned, was there by God's will, and had the duty to rule according to God's ordinance. That duty also conferred certain rights, but the monarch essentially held a position of supreme responsibility that should not be abused. Elizabeth did not take kindly to any challenge to her position of privilege and authority; she reacted strongly against overt threats to her position and she fought powerful rearguard action against threats that might come from within Parliament and the Church. The appeal of more radical Protestantism had all sorts of alternative implications; besides the notion of the theocratic clergy was the basis for a reformed society, a society in which many of the old hierarchical values would be set aside forever. It is possible to look at the rise of militant Protestantism in this period and see it as a revolutionary movement, as a shift from the old medieval order towards a new more democratic vision of society, and it is significant that so many of the early settlers in the New World were Protestant refugees seeking the space in which to worship what was denied them in their own lands. There must have been times when Elizabeth saw the threats to her authority as encroaching on her like the two claws of a huge scorpion: one pincer being the Catholic Church from which she had moved away, with its attendant allies in southern Europe and Ireland, and the other the radical Protestant sects threatening her from within her own Parliament and her own country, accusing her of having failed to carry out the necessary reforms in which she had placed her hopes.

Elizabeth's position, therefore, became more reactionary as she gauged the measure of the forces lining up against her. A liberal by nature, she was forced to take a harsher stand, thereby confirming the views of her opposition who saw her as a Jezebel, a woman whose hands were stained with the blood of martyrs of varying faiths.

Her own faith was unquestionable, even though her beliefs were more ambiguous. In all the analyses of her political tactics and her battles with the Puritans in Parliament, relatively little attention is given to her own private devotional practices. We know that she attended services daily in her private chapel and that she enjoyed the beauty of ritual language, music and use of vestments. We know also that she believed in religious tolerance and can therefore be described as a woman with broad religious views. Besides this, details of some prayers composed by Elizabeth in several languages and written in the tiny prayer book that she is said to have used from 1579 onwards show a slightly different picture of the Queen at prayer.

Characteristic of the prayers is the humility expressed in them. Elizabeth confides herself to God, confesses that her power resides in his permission to her to use it, admits her own weaknesses and asks for help in a dangerous world. The image of the changing wheel of fortune returns again, and one prayer especially, written in English, draws on her own life story, becoming a powerfully moving personal statement:

> Of nothing hast thou made me, not a worm, but a Creature according to thine own image, heaping all the blessings upon me that men on earth hold most happy, Drawing my blood from Kings and my bringing up in virtue, giving me that [which] more is, even in my youth, knowledge of thy truth and in times of most danger, most gracious deliverance; pulling me from the prison to the palace and placing me a Sovereign Princess over thy people of England. And above all this making me, (though a weak woman) yet thy instrument, to set forth the glorious Gospel of thy dear Son, Jesus Christ. Thus in these last and worst days of the world, when wars and seditions with grievous persecutions have vexed almost all Kings and Countries round about me, my reign hath been peacable, and my Realm a receptacle to the afflicted church. The love of my people hath appeared firm, and the devices of mine enemies frustrate. Now for these and other thy benefits, (Oh Lord of all goodness) what have I rendered to thee? Forgetfulness, unthankfulness and great disobedience. I should have magnified thee. I have neglected thee. I should have prayed unto thee. I have forgotten thee. I should have served thee. I have sinned against thee. This is my case.[19]

There is an energy and an intensity in this prayer, as in the others bound in this Prayer Book, that sound like the authentic voice of Elizabeth. Whenever her emotions were highly charged, in anger, grief, love or enthusiasm, her use of language reflects that dynamism. In this prayer, meditating upon her worldly success and her own personal inadequacy, an image emerges of a woman well aware of her own shortcomings and, for that moment at least, repentant of her faults; even though she had no intention of changing them once she left the atmosphere of her private chapel. The voice in these prayers seems to be a combination of self-assertion and self-abasement, saying 'here I am, this is how you made me, but I wish things could be otherwise'. In that respect, the ambiguity expressed in Elizabeth's prayers could well be taken as the most revealing statement about her attitude to life.

Notes

1. Letter from Count de Feria to Philip II, quoted in Mumby, *The Girlhood of Queen Elizabeth* (London: Constable, 1909), pp. 322–5.
2. Letter from John Jewel to Peter Martyr, 20 March 1559, quoted ibid., pp. 325–7.
3. Paul Johnson, *Elizabeth: A Study in Power and Intellect* (London: Weidenfeld & Nicolson, 1974), p. 88.
4. Letter from Elizabeth to the deprived bishops, 6 December 1559, repr. in G. B. Harrison, *The Letters of Queen Elizabeth* (London: Cassell, 1935), pp. 29–31.
5. Johnson, *Elizabeth*, p. 89.
6. Edward Rishton's Continuation of Nicolas Sanders's *Rise and Growth of the Anglican Schism*, trans. and ed. David Lewis (London: 1877; orig. pub. Cologne, 1585) in Richard L. Greaves (ed.), *Elizabeth I, Queen of England* (Lexington, Mass: D. C. Heath, 1974), pp. 21–6.
7. Christopher Haigh, 'The Church of England, The Catholics and the People', in idem (ed.), *The Reign of Elizabeth I* (London: Macmillan, 1984), pp. 195–219.
8. Philip Hughes, *The Reformation in England*, in Greaves, *Queen of England*, pp. 149–55.
9. Arnold Oskar Meyer, *England and the Catholic Church under Queen Elizabeth*, trans. Rev. J. R. McKee (London: Routledge & Kegan Paul, 1915, reissued 1967) p. 181.

10. Ibid., p. 300.
11. Johnson, *Elizabeth*, p. 349.
12. Quoted ibid., p.349.
13. Jean-Louis Barrault, *Rabelais: A Dramatic Game*, trans. Robert Baldick, (London: Faber & Faber, 1971).
14. Sir Henry Sidney, quoted in J. B. Black, *The Reign of Elizabeth 1558–1603*, (Oxford: Clarendon Press, 1936), p. 391.
15. Sir Henry Sidney, quoted in Johnson, *Elizabeth*, p. 379.
16. Letter from Elizabeth to the Lord Justices Loftus and Gardner, the Earl of Ormonde and the rest of the Council of Ireland, 12 September 1598, repr. in Harrison, *Letters*, pp. 260–3.
17. Letter from Elizabeth to Henri IV, King of France, repr. ibid., p. 225.
18. Quoted in J. E. Neale, *Elizabeth I and her Parliaments* (London: Jonathan Cape, 1957), pp. 69–71.
19. English prayer by Elizabeth, quoted in Frederick Chamberlin, *The Sayings of Queen Elizabeth* (London: John Lane, Bodley Head, 1923), pp. 107–9.

6 Public Statement, Private Crisis

Of all the episodes in Elizabeth's long and interesting life, two in particular have caught the imagination of innumerable writers, artists and composers. The Dudley affair, for all the mileage it supplied to romantic novelists, changed its nature quite early in Elizabeth's reign, and whatever passion may or may not have been there when both were in their twenties had turned into a profound friendship a decade later. Elizabeth continued to flirt openly with Dudley and to heap unusual honours and privileges upon him. It was widely speculated that she also allowed him to share her bed, but after the death of Dudley's wife Amy Robsart the possibility of marriage disintegrated and the relationship that remained until Dudley's death as a fat, white-haired, red-faced, middle-aged man no longer caught the romantic imagination.

The same cannot be said, however, for the relationships between Elizabeth and Mary Stuart and between Elizabeth and Dudley's stepson Robert Devereux the second Earl of Essex. Both have supplied material for novels, poems, plays, operas, paintings, ballads and, in the twentieth century, films, and the interest generated by both these relationships appears to be perennial. Certainly, there is much documentary evidence on which to construct an account of the exchanges between Elizabeth and Mary and between Elizabeth and Essex; there are letters, testimonies from witnesses and, of course, accounts of the executions of both Mary and Essex, though the accounts differ widely according to the point of view of the observer. What makes these relationships eternally fascinating, however, is that both contain all the ingredients of the romantic adventure story, each with its own special variants. The Elizabeth and Mary story is most often presented in terms of a conflict between Queens, two powerful (and, in some versions, beautiful and jealous) women engaged in a struggle for supremacy that lasted for over thirty years and finally ended in the destruction of one woman by the other. Threads running through this basic tale include love stories (did Mary have an affair with Babington, as some nineteenth century versions of the story suggest?), the plotting of one Queen to overthrow the other, religious warfare, and personal competition between two women. A common device of those using the Mary –Elizabeth material has been to invent a meeting between the two women in which both Queens match their strength verbally and express their hatred of one another. The powerful second act of Donizetti's opera *Maria Stuarda* contains just such an encounter, between an arrogant, red-haired Elizabeth dressed in her favourite white gown, and a proud, imprisoned but unbowed Mary, wearing the colour she adopted as a sign of her deprivation, deepest black.

The Elizabeth and Essex story contains similar ingredients — plotting, civil unrest, a powerful woman and a wild, passionate young man. But here the age difference between the two provides an added ingredient. Elizabeth is generally portrayed as an embittered older (very old) woman, in love with a man young enough to be her grandson and choosing finally to have him executed out of spite, when she realises the hopelessness of her position. The famous incident when Essex returned unexpectedly from Ireland in 1599 and surprised Elizabeth in her bedchamber has been a rich source of inspiration for a good many writers. Rowland Whyte describes what actually took place:

> On Michaelmas Eve, about ten o'clock in the morning, Lord Essex lighted at Court Gate Post, made all haste up to the Presence, and so to the Privy Chamber, and stayed not until he came to the Queen's Bedchamber, where he found the Queen, newly up, her hair about her face; he kneeled unto her, kissed her hands, and had some private speech with her, which seemed to give him great contentment; for coming from her Majesty to go shift himself in his chamber, he was very pleasant, and thanked God that, though he had suffered much troubles, and storms abroad, he found a sweet calm home. 'Tis much wondered at here that he went so boldly to her Majesty's presence, she not being ready, and he so full of dirt and mire, that his very face was full of it. When ready he went up again for half an hour after twelve. As yet all was well, and her usage very gracious towards him.[1]

The image of the old Queen, startled in the privacy of her inner sanctum, without her wigs, make-up and jewellery is one that has come down through the centuries, giving fuel to the idea that

Elizabeth acted out of frustrated vanity in disposing of her young favourite. But in fact, as in the case of Mary Stuart, the romanticised versions of Elizabeth's problematic relationship with the man she perhaps saw as the son she might have had with Robert Dudley are a long way from the rather more pragmatic reality. Rowland Whyte wondered at Elizabeth's leniency with Essex; in fact such a gesture was absolutely typical. Elizabeth must have seen that Essex was desperate; she might have thought that he had come to take her prisoner and stage a *coup d'état*. Until she could be certain as to the meaning of his behaviour she behaved in a conciliatory manner and showed outward good humour and calm. Later in the day, Whyte records, Essex went back to see the Queen and 'he found her much changed'. He was ordered to be confined to his own room and when he was finally set free, he was banned from court and from any form of public employment. From then it was a steady process of decline, as Essex refused to recognise his altered status and finally staged his abortive revolt, which resulted in his execution in 1601, less than eighteen months after his invasion of Elizabeth's bedchamber. Whatever private pain this caused Elizabeth, she acted with her usual cunning and courage when faced with the crisis that he generated. The weak-minded, foolish old woman of fiction is a long way from the shrewd, quick-thinking monarch who acted with speed and common sense to save herself from what might so easily have been an attempt to overthrow her.

The conflict between Elizabeth and Mary Stuart began when Elizabeth came to the throne in 1558. Mary Stuart was then sixteen years old, living at the French court and married to the French Dauphin François. The day after Elizabeth's coronation, Mary and François adopted the style of King and Queen of England and included the English royal arms in Mary's shield. From the very start of Elizabeth's reign, therefore, Mary stated her intentions to proclaim her right to the English throne in lieu of Elizabeth. Mary's claim derived from her direct descent, like Elizabeth, from Henry VII. Henry VIII's elder sister, Margaret, had married the Scottish King, James IV. Their son James V married the French princess Marie de Guise, and their daughter was Mary Stuart. Mary's claim to the English throne was therefore virtually identical to that of the ill-fated Lady Jane Grey, grand-daughter of Henry VIII's younger sister Mary. The difference between the Scottish and English branches of the family was principally a matter of religion; the Stuarts were Catholics while Mary Tudor's descendants, like Elizabeth herself, were Protestants. During her reign Elizabeth took care to neutralise the threat of a claimant to her throne emerging from the Grey family, and always kept a watchful eye on her Grey cousins Catherine and Mary, whom she seems to have disliked personally, regardless of the potential threat they or their descendants might have posed to her.

With Mary Stuart, however, the case was different. Mary was not a subordinate courtier but a woman with a claim to the Scottish throne and a husband who in July 1559 succeeded to the throne of France. Marie of Guise, Mary's mother, was Regent of Scotland in her daughter's absence, and in 1559 a revolt began against her, fuelled by the spread of the Reformation in Scotland and powerful anti-Catholic feeling. Marie of Guise was deposed and the Scottish Protestant nobility appealed to Elizabeth for help. Elizabeth began her reign with the Scottish crisis a major thorn in her side.

The Scottish rebellion caused Elizabeth grave problems. If she supported the Scottish Protestant cause openly she would be perceived by the French to be acting illegally and could well arouse French aggression in retaliation. On the other hand, not to act was to risk French intervention in the Scottish conflict on the Catholic side, which, with Mary Stuart already claiming the English throne as her own right, was a very dangerous prospect. Caught between France to the south and a pro-French Scotland to the north, England would be trapped in a narrow wedge between the two. Elizabeth acted with her usual common sense and cunning and intervened in Scotland by subterfuge. Secret transactions involving money, supplies and military assistance flowed across the Border, though in public Elizabeth flatly denied that anything of the kind was going on. Then in 1560, when the Scottish conflict had grown bitter beyond repair, Elizabeth agreed to direct intervention and sent an army into Scotland. This time, however, her tactics worked, and when the Treaty of Edinburgh finally brought peace in July 1560, one of the conditions laid down and agreed upon by the Scots was that Mary and François, the absentee monarchs, should give up their claim to the English throne and cease using the English royal coat of arms.

These terms, imposed upon Mary and François, were rejected by them, but before open conflict between the ruler and the Scottish nobility could occur, François died and Mary was left a widow at nineteen years of age. With no future for her in France she decided to return to Scotland and take on the duties of reigning Scottish queen. Sir John Neale summarises the situation between the two Queens at this point:

> The crowding drama of Elizabeth's reign changed, and interest began to centre on the personal relations between herself and Mary, two young queens, cousins and neighbours. What was to be expected but restless enmity? Elizabeth had as good as robbed Mary of the allegiance of her subjects, and set up a religious and political rule in Scotland that was obnoxious to her. Mary on her side had refused to ratify the Treaty of Edinburgh, and, given the will and power, could take a leaf out her rival's book, stir up Catholic discontent in England, perhaps make a bid for the English throne. There was a provocation and danger in her very widowhood, for she could challenge her cousin's attractions as the best marriage in Europe. Suitors who had spent money, time and temper on Elizabeth, were turning to woo a woman less virginal and elusive, and it was not many weeks before the names of Don Carlos of Spain, the Archduke Charles, the King of Sweden, and the King of Denmark were on people's lips. With Elizabeth it was political necessity — perhaps it was also instinct — to begrudge another her half or wholly rejected suitors.[2]

The tone of Neale's account of the situation at the time of Mary's return to Scotland provides a good example of the way in which historians, let alone writers of fiction, have perceived the conflict between Elizabeth and Mary in sexist terms. Two women, it is assumed, must be enemies, they must be rivals, they must be somehow engaged in competition for suitors against one another. So much of the writing about the relationship between Elizabeth and Mary has been in similar terms, and it all follows the widespread myth that enmity between women is a more natural state of affairs than friendship. Certainly there was little possibility of friendship between two women who differed so widely on practically everything as did Elizabeth and Mary, but it is over-simplistic to perceive the conflict between them in terms of competition for sexual supremacy. The disagreements were on other levels: religious, political and, ultimately, intellectual.

Elizabeth had received an extensive Humanist education; she had studied classical authors and had as good a background in the new learning as any man of her age. Her intellectual prowess was something on which she prided herself and, as has already been seen, she continued to work at her translations and to read widely throughout her life. Mary, on the other hand, had received a different kind of education. The emphasis on women's scholarship that had been so pronounced at the court of Henry VIII had not been an essential part of her upbringing. Her languages were limited to a knowledge of Latin, French and English and she did not have anything like the breadth of learning acquired and sustained by Elizabeth. She was, as her life story reveals, a very brave woman, with tremendous stamina and physical resilience. She also seems to have been very quick-thinking, often to her own detriment when she acted without taking heed of the possible consequences. The contrast between Elizabeth's careful treading of a middle path, designed to confound anyone who tried to make her admit to a precise position, and Mary's hasty actions is marked. Terms such as 'headstrong, impetuous, emotional, indomitable' fill the pages of romantic biographers of Mary Stuart, and these qualities are often contrasted with Elizabeth's circumspection to the detriment of the English Queen.

Nevertheless, when Mary finally returned to Scotland, having travelled by sea rather than apply to cross English territory, she too adopted a cautious position in the early stages. Although a devout Catholic, she had sense enough to see the strength of Protestant feeling around her at the court and took pains to be seen as a moderate. Her own religious position was perfectly clear. 'I am none of those that will change my religion every year', she is reputed to have said, but she acknowledged the right to alternative modes of worship. When she formed her council of twelve lords she included both Catholics and staunch Protestants and began her reign with the appearance of harmony that belied her most savage critics, such as John Knox, author of the aforementioned misogynous tract that had so angered Elizabeth, *The First Blast of the Trumpet against the Monstrous Regiment of Women* (1558) in which he declared that 'God hath revealed to some in this our age that it is more than a monster in nature that a woman should reign and bear empire above man'.

The accession of Mary to the Scottish throne led to an increase in diplomatic transactions between Scotland and England, as Elizabeth demanded that Mary recognise the Treaty of Edinburgh and Mary, slightly modifying her position, sought to be designated as Elizabeth's successor. Still enmeshed in marriage negotiations of various kinds, Elizabeth was reluctant to name anyone as her successor, let alone a Catholic Queen of a neighbouring state. Mary also began the search for a suitable husband, and until 1565, when she finally married her cousin, Henry Lord Darnley, the question of Mary's marriage preoccupied Elizabeth as much as that of her own.

Mary stated unequivocally that she would never marry a Protestant, and further, that she would not accept a husband chosen for her by Elizabeth. Elizabeth, for her part, was anxious that Mary should not marry anyone who might increase the threat to her own stability on the English throne. For a time negotiations were under way for a marriage to Philip II's mentally unstable son Don Carlos,[3] but it is doubtful whether this was ever a serious proposition. Mary began secret negotiations regarding a marriage to Lord Darnley, and Elizabeth made the extraordinary gesture of ennobling Robert Dudley, making him Earl of Leicester and offering him to the Scottish Queen as a possible husband.

The suggestion of a marriage between Mary Stuart and Robert Dudley was held up as a possibility for more than a year, during which time Mary expressed her resentment at such a proposition and Dudley himself appears to have been less than enthusiastic. There has been a great deal of speculation as to whether Elizabeth was serious in making such a suggestion; since Dudley was at that time a strong contender for her own affections, and had still not given up hope of marrying her despite the Amy Robsart scandal, it is often assumed that Elizabeth's proposition was simply a delaying tactic. Another reading of the situation perceives Elizabeth's gesture as consciously insulting to Mary, an act calculated to make her react by marrying someone Elizabeth considered totally unsuitable. Elizabeth has sometimes been depicted as completely Machiavellian, in that her suggestion of Dudley as a husband for Mary was merely a stage in her ultimate plot, which was to drive Mary into the arms of the totally inadequate Henry Darnley. Certainly Mary decided to marry Darnley with some speed, shortly after he was allowed to leave England and travel to Edinburgh, ostensibly to visit his father.

Conyers Read, who believes that Elizabeth was serious in wanting the marriage between Mary and Dudley, is nevertheless puzzled by Elizabeth's decision to allow Darnley to go to Scotland. Darnley himself could be considered as a claimant to the English throne, being descended from the widowed Queen Margaret of Scotland, Mary's grandmother, through her second marriage to the Earl of Angus. Darnley's mother the Countess of Lennox, whom Elizabeth detested, made no secret of her pretensions and it is unlikely that Elizabeth would have looked favourably on the marriage. The suggestion that Elizabeth might have plotted the Darnley–Mary marriage is based on a theory developed after the collapse of the marriage and Darnley's death, it being assumed that Elizabeth had some magical knowledge of future events, which is of course nonsensical. What seems far more likely is that Dudley himself intervened since he secretly favoured Darnley's cause. Read points out that Leicester told the Scottish envoy Sir James Melville that he did not aspire himself to Mary's hand, and that 'the invention of that proposition proceeded from Mr. Cecil, his secret enemy'.[4] Leicester may well have informed Mary that the suggestion of himself as husband was a deliberate ploy on Elizabeth's and Cecil's part to dissuade her from marrying Darnley, thus releasing himself from the difficult position of being proposed as husband to one Queen by the Queen he wanted to marry himself.

Mary married Darnley in July 1565, and proclaimed him King of Scotland. Within weeks she had come to regret the marriage bitterly. A report sent to Dudley in February 1566, painted a gloomy picture of the situation in Scotland. 'I know now for certain that this Queen repenteth her marriage; that she hateth the King and all his kin. . . . David, with the consent of the King, shall have his throat cut within ten days. Many things grievouser and worse than these are brought to my ears, yes, of things intended against her own person.'[5] The David referred to in this letter was David Rizzio, Mary's secretary and close confidant. The relationship between Rizzio and Mary was indeed so close that rumour circulated that Mary's increasingly obvious pregnancy might be the result of their liaison, rather than of the short-lived marriage of the drunken, debauched young Darnley. Hatred of Rizzio came from all sides, not only from Darnley and his supporters but also from the Protestant nobility around Mary who resented his influence. In March 1566 while dining with Mary at Holyrood House, Rizzio was brutally murdered in front of her. Concealing her loathing of her husband, who had been responsible in large part for the outrage, Mary persuaded him to desert his fellow conspirators and managed to escape from Holyrood. The resilience shown by both Mary and Elizabeth in times of crisis and threat of mortal danger is remarkable; they may have been very different people in temperament and training, but they shared a courage and ability for quick thinking that more than once enabled them to survive.

Mary's son, the future James VI of Scotland and I of England was born in June 1566. Elizabeth agreed to be godmother to the new prince, and the Spanish ambassador reported that Elizabeth told him that she would have taken Darnley's dagger and stabbed him with it herself, had she been subjected to the kind of monstrous behaviour as that occasioned by the murder of Rizzio. But the brief phase of good will did not last. Mary harboured resentment against Darnley and had fallen in love with the Earl of Bothwell. The Mary–Bothwell story, which has also supplied material for an abundance of fictionalised accounts of the relationship, seems to have been a genuine case of extreme passion on Mary's part. Though still married to Darnley, and knowing that Bothwell was married also, Mary wrote passionate letters and poems to Bothwell, and seems to have believed that she could have a future with him. There is some suggestion that the relationship between Mary and Bothwell was a sado-masochistic one, having begun with Mary's rape by the man who was outspokenly contemptuous of women. Whatever the truth of the relationship, Bothwell and by implication Mary were involved in the scandal that finally brought Mary down and led to her removal from the throne. In February 1567, Darnley, who was recovering from smallpox, was found murdered. The house in which he was lodged in Edinburgh was blown up and his body was found in an adjoining garden. The corpse did not show signs of having been blown to pieces in the explosion, however, but of having been strangled. There was no question but that Darnley had been murdered.

Elizabeth wrote to Mary on hearing the news. It is a short, strongly worded letter, and it contains some sound advice from one woman to another. Elizabeth's concern in this letter is principally for Mary:

> My ears have been so astounded and my heart so frightened to hear of the horrible and abominable muder of your husband and my own cousin that I have scarcely spirit to write; yet I cannot conceal that I grieve more for you than for him. I should not do the office of a faithful cousin and friend, if I did not urge you to preserve your honour, rather than look through your fingers at revenge on those who have done you that pleasure as most people say. I counsel you so to take this matter to heart, that you may show the world what a noble Princess and loyal woman you are. I write thus vehemently not that I doubt, but for affection.[6]

Elizabeth's advice fell upon deaf ears. Mary proceeded to marry Bothwell and a month after their marriage, he was a fugitive and she a prisoner. Elizabeth wrote again:

> Madam, to be plain with you, our grief hath not been small that in this your marriage no slender consideration has been had that, as we perceive manifestly no good friend you have in the whole world can like thereof, and, if we should otherwise write or say, we should abuse you. For how could a worse choice be made for your honour than in such haste to marry a subject who, besides other notorious lacks, public fame hath charged with the murder of your late husband, besides the touching of yourself in some part, though we trust in that behalf falsely. And with what peril have you married him, that hath another lawful wife alive, whereby neither by God's law nor man's yourself can be his lawful wife nor any children betwixt you legitimate?[7]

Elizabeth's analysis of Mary's plight in these letters is a very personal one. Concern for her own honour had always been of great importance, and she must have assumed that Mary would share the same priorities. In fact, the opposite was true. Mary's passion for Bothwell was so overwhelmingly strong, that it imposed itself over all other considerations. Brought into Edinburgh as a prisoner, with the crowds calling her a whore and a witch

110

and screaming for her to be burned, Mary swore she would have them all hanged and crucified. She was deposed and her brother established as ruler in her place. Pregnant, she miscarried twins and finally in 1568 escaped from the island prison of Loch Leven and crossed into England, a penniless refugee, throwing herself on the mercy of her ruling cousin Elizabeth.

The long imprisonment of the Queen of Scots in England, from her arrival in 1568 to her death in 1587 marks another stage in the relationship between Mary and Elizabeth. Though Mary lived in various parts of England, the two women never met. Elizabeth was anxious for Mary's complicity in Darnley's murder not to be proven, but was equally anxious to prevent Mary from gaining a ground base of support among the Catholic nobility in England. When the Northern Rising took place in 1569 and it became clear that Mary was going to go on plotting for her own release and for Elizabeth's throne, it became impossible for Elizabeth ever to allow Mary her freedom. After the discovery of the Ridolfi Plot, Mary was placed under specially close arrest and wrote angrily to Elizabeth to complain. Elizabeth wrote back, restraining her own emotions:

> But now finding by your last letter on the 27th of the last an increase of your impatience, tending also to uncomely, passionate, ireful and vindictive speeches, I thought to change my former opinion, and by patient and advised words to move you to stay or qualify your passions, and to consider that it is not the manner to obtain good things with evil speeches, nor benefits with injurious challenges, or to conclude, all in one word, good to yourself, with doing evil to myself.[8]

The long imprisonment of Mary in England did not prevent her from constantly taking part in schemes for her release and for a Catholic ruler on the English throne. Mary's singlemindedness reflects the narrow confines of the world in which she was compelled to live, and as she plotted with emissaries from Spain and disaffected Catholics she failed to realise how far conditions in the world outside had changed. Elizabeth's years on the throne had given her insight into the machinations of foreign diplomacy; she had steered a careful course of moderation, had successfully come through the one serious attempt to overthrow her, and had managed to keep England from open war with Spain. Nevertheless, she was always aware of that threat, and, as the situation in Europe deteriorated and the English economy became more unstable, Elizabeth came to rely on the efficient security network set up for her in the 1570s by Walsingham. Walsingham himself was quite clear that Elizabeth should act to remove Mary: writing to Leicester in 1572 he stated simply: 'So long as that devilish woman lives neither her Majesty must make account to continue in quiet possession of her crown, nor her faithful servants assure themselves of safety of their lives.'[9] Walsingham's spy network exposed several plots involving Mary, but Elizabeth made no move to act against her. She was reluctant to condemn another monarch, and resisted all calls on her to have Mary executed. Then in the 1580s, with the Spanish menace growing larger and the seminary priests operating clandestinely through England and Ireland, matters accelerated out of Elizabeth's control. A serious plot was uncovered in 1583, and two Catholic gentlemen, Lord Henry Howard and Francis Throckmorton, revealed under torture that the conspiracy also had international support. Then in 1586 came the Babington Plot, in which the devious Walsingham set up a young Catholic supporter of Mary's, Anthony Babington, and managed to obtain letters from Mary that proved her complicity in a plot to kill Elizabeth. Babington and six fellow conspirators were arrested, hanged, drawn and quartered, and the way was now clear for Mary to be tried and executed. Elizabeth prevaricated, dodged and wove her way through the mounting demands on her to have Mary put to death. To the deputation from Parliament, urging her to carry out sentence of death on Mary, she answered:

> And now though my life hath been dangerously shot at, yet I protest there is nothing hath more grieved me, than that one not differing from me in sex, of like rank and degree, of the same stock, and most nearly allied unto me in blood, hath fallen into so great a crime. . . . And even yet, though the matter be come thus far, if she would truly repent, and no man would undertake her cause against me, and if my life alone depended hereupon, and not the safety and welfare of my whole people, I would, (I protest unfeignedly) most willingly pardon her.[10]

Pardon was an impossibility. Pressure on Elizabeth came from all sides, reinforced by her own anxieties about the growing threat of a Spanish invasion. In October 1586, she wrote bluntly to Mary:

> You have in various ways and manners attempted to take my life and to bring my kingdom to destruction by bloodshed. I have never proceeded so harshly against you, but have, on the contrary, protected and maintained you like myself. These treasons will be proved to you and all made manifest. Yet it is my will, that you answer the nobles and peers of the kingdom as if I were myself present. I therefore require, charge and command that you make answer for I have been well informed of your arrogance. Act plainly without reserve, and you will sooner be able to obtain favour from me.[11]

Mary was executed at Fotheringay Castle on 7 February 1587. She died bravely, proclaiming her belief in the Roman Catholic faith. It was noted that she looked unhealthy, had put on a lot of weight (though being six feet tall she could no doubt stand it) and her hair had gone grey. The once-famous beauty of the Scottish Queen was quite gone. Elizabeth reacted badly to the news of Mary's death, accusing her counsellors of disloyalty, claiming she had never meant the death warrant to be carried out and ordering Cecil away from court, temporarily, calling him a traitor and false dissembler.

Mary Stuart was forty-four years old when she died. Elizabeth was ten years older at that date and in quite good health, aside from the chronic state of her teeth which we have already referred to. The crisis of Mary Stuart's trial and execution, however, put Elizabeth under tremendous strain; her handwriting, normally remarkable for its beauty and legibility, was almost unreadable during the period leading up to the execution, a fact which bears witness to her state of mind. After Mary's death a series of other crises further disturbed her life — the arrival and defeat of the Spanish Armada, the death of Robert Dudley Earl of Leicester, her long standing confidant, and the ongoing problems in Ireland. As her old friends died, Elizabeth became more isolated. The French ambassador described her in the 1590s in less than flattering terms:

> She was strangely attired in a dress of silver cloth, white and crimson, or silver 'gauze' as they call it. This dress had slashed

sleeves lined with red taffeta, and was girt about with other little sleeves that hung down to the ground, which she was forever twisting and untwisting. She kept the front of her dress open, and one could see the whole of her bosom, and passing low, and often she would open the front of this robe with her hands, as if she was too hot . . . . On her head she wore a garland . . . and beneath it a great reddish coloured wig, with a great number of pearls, not of great worth. On either side of her ears hung two great curls of hair, almost down to her shoulders and within the collar of her robe, spangled like the top of her head. Her bosom is somewhat wrinkled. . . . As for her face, it is and appears to be very aged. It is long and thin, and her teeth are very yellow and irregular . . . many of them are missing, so that one cannot understand her easily when she speaks.[12]

It is perhaps understandable that at such a point in her life Elizabeth should have been drawn to an image of youthfulness, particularly when the bearer of the image was closely linked to Robert Dudley. Robert Devereux Earl of Essex was the son by her first husband of Lettice Knollys, Elizabeth's once detested competitor and second wife of Dudley. Essex had been educated in Cecil's household, and was brought to court by Dudley in 1584. By 1587 he was such a favourite with the Queen that eyewitnesses reported that she sat up all night with him playing cards. Some months later she made him her Master of the Horse.

Many romantic biographers have treated the relationship between Elizabeth and Essex as one between lovers. She bought the favours of a young, handsome man, he paid for his preferment at court by obliging an ageing woman. Some element of this may have been present, but it seems more likely that the sexual dimension was completely absent. Elizabeth originally received Essex in her company as a favour to Dudley, and quickly found him an entertaining companion. All her life she enjoyed the company of people of energy and charm, and Essex seems to have had both. He also had disadvantages; he was reckless, arrogant and incapable of listening to advice. He seems to have behaved with Elizabeth like a small boy with a doting parent, and she tolerated many of his excesses for longer than most commentators would have expected. Nevertheless, rather than being gulled by Essex, she seems to have seen through him, and her treatment of him was a combination of cynicism and affection. To Bacon, who commented on Essex's extravagant flattery of her, she remarked: 'Essex has written me some dutiful letters, which moved me; but after taking them to flow from the abundance of his heart, I find them but a preparative to a suit for renewing his farm of sweet wines.'[13]

Elizabeth was always a practical woman, with a hard head for business. When Essex began to lose her money through abortive voyages overseas, she began to lose patience. In July 1598, driven beyond endurance by his rudeness when he turned his back on her, she slapped him across the face in public. His response was to go for his sword, and he had to be bundled out of the room to escape Elizabeth's fury.

Essex's position was not easy. The court in the 1590s was a turbulent place, filled with ambitious young men, all being promoted by their respective sponsors and vying with one another for the Queen's special favour. Sir Walter Raleigh was such a man, as was Francis Bacon, and Robert Cecil, son of Elizabeth's most trusted adviser, was another. Essex saw himself as a rival to such men, and even while they competed with each other for attentions from Elizabeth, many of the younger courtiers kept a watchful and attentive eye on Scotland, where James VI bided his time, waiting for the old Queen to die. It cannot have been a comfortable period in Elizabeth's life, and though some of the more extreme pictures painted — of the Queen living among corrupt courtiers, an over-made-up, senile old harridan — are unfair, Elizabeth was ageing rapidly and her temper, by all accounts, was wearing very thin indeed. Essex, on the other hand, young and arrogant, was the sort of person to create around himself a cluster of followers. Bacon described him as 'a man of nature not to be ruled', adding that he had a popular reputation and insufficient means for his greatness. He questioned whether there could be a more dangerous companion for any monarch, particularly to a woman of Elizabeth's taste and temperament. For Essex's ambitions, financial in the first instance, were growing all the time.

In 1598 Elizabeth unpredictably gave him the post of command in Ireland. Quite why she did this remains mysterious, but Essex had been taking a great interest in Irish affairs for several years and Elizabeth was anxious to have the Irish revolt suppressed as quickly and as efficiently as possible. As with her decision to send Robert Dudley to the Low Countries, she seems to have made an error of judgement. Unaware of the precise conditions of leading an army in the field, she allowed herself to be guided, perhaps, by abstract ideals of what a knight commander should be, rather than by practical considerations. Essex accepted the Irish appointment with some misgivings, perhaps because he realised that it was of crucial importance to him; if he failed in Ireland, his unstable relationship with Elizabeth would finally collapse.

Essex did fail in Ireland. Elizabeth sent precise orders as to how she wanted the campaign to be conducted, and Essex ignored them. Elizabeth's letters, long and detailed, show considerable patience and forbearance; her usually aggressive letter-writing is slightly muted, and the tone, as she reproves Essex for his conduct of the campaign, his wastefulness, his missed opportunities could be described as one of constrained tolerance. The anger runs under the surface, but she seems to have bent over backwards to give Essex more rope. Finally, on 17 September 1599, when she learned that Essex had spoken personally with the rebel leader Tyrone and agreed to a truce in direct contradiction of her orders, she wrote again:

> It appeareth by your journal that you and the traitor spoke half an hour together, without anybody's hearing; wherein, though we that trust you with our kingdom are far from mistrusting you with a traitor, yet both for comeliness, example, and your own discharge, we marvel you would carry it no better; especially having in all things since your arrival been so precise to have good testimony for your actions, as whenever anything was to be done to which our commandment tied you, it seemed sufficient warrant for you if your fellow councillors allowed better of other ways, though your own reason carried you to have pursued our directions against their opinions.[14]

The letter concludes with a warning to Essex not to grant Tyrone a pardon without having first received written authority from the Queen. Elizabeth was obviously beginning to suspect Essex of wanting more than military success and financial grandeur.

The letter was not answered. Instead, Essex crossed to England, leaving his command, and, in that celebrated incident referred to above, confronted the Queen in her own bedchamber. Confined to his room and under house arrest for a time, Essex effectively lost his hold on Elizabeth after that point, but it is recorded that when he fell ill she sent him her own doctors and some nourishing broth, proving that she still took an affectionate interest in his fortunes. Recovered, Essex set out once again on improving his lot; this time he indulged in a more dangerous conspiracy. Whether his mind was slightly unhinged at this time is not clear, but his actions certainly suggest it. He seems to have believed that Elizabeth was senile and that she was completely in the grip of Robert Cecil and his cronies. In February 1601, Essex rode out with 200 supporters heading for the City of London and claiming that a plot had been laid against his life. He met no support and was duly arrested. Elizabeth commented to the French ambassador that 'a senseless ingrate' had at last revealed what had been in his mind all along.

Essex, together with his comrade the Earl of Southampton, whose close association with Shakespeare casts interesting light on Shakespeare's proclivity for writing plays dealing with problems of kingliness and king-making, was brought to trial a week after his arrest. He was condemned to death, along with a number of other conspirators, though only a small number were actually executed. Southampton was one of those spared. One of the romantic versions of Essex's death is that he tried to send Elizabeth a ring that she had given him if he ever needed her forgiveness, but that one of his enemies took it and did not pass it on to the Queen. Like so much else in the Essex–Elizabeth story, this is another invention, but it is part of the legend that has grown up around the unfortunate episode of Essex's death.

After his execution Elizabeth is said to have mentioned his name on various occasions and she wore a ring he had given her until she died, but the whole sorry business had depressed and embittered her. Essex was recorded in popular ballads as 'the valiant knight of chivalry', while Sir John Harington, the Queen's beloved godson, records that she was seriously troubled in body and in mind:

She is much disfavoured and unattired, and these troubles waste her much. She disregardeth every costly cover that cometh to the table, and taketh little but manchet and succory potage. Every new message from the City doth disturb her, and she frowns on all the ladies. . . . She walks much in her Privy Chamber, and stamps with her feet at ill news, and thrust her rusty sword at times into the arras in great rage. My Lord Buckhurst is much with her, and few else since the City business; but the dangers are over, and yet she always keeps a sword by her table.[15]

Harington's letter is an account of how Elizabeth was becoming more and more melancholy and withdrawn, more paranoid than at any time in her life and showing signs in public of acute depression. There is something very sad about the accounts of her last months, as healthy, ambitious men moving their crafty way through court politics presided over the gradual decline of an old woman. When she died, Elizabeth had finally succumbed to depression. Refusing to eat, she sat for hours on her cushions on the floor, as her sister Mary had done before her death half a century earlier. When finally persuaded to go to bed, she lay for some days more, with Whitgift and other clergy at her side, taking care to ensure that she would die with her obligations fulfilled in the sight of God. On 24 March, after a night of heavy rain, Elizabeth died. Her favourite chaplain, Dr Parry, was at her bedside. Dying, she was at least with a few people who appear to have cared for her: 'This morning about three o'clock her Majesty departed this life, mildly like a lamb, easily like a ripe apple from the tree. . . . Dr Parry told me he was present, and sent his prayers before her soul; and I doubt not but she is amongst the royal saints in heaven in eternal joys'.[16]

Notes

1. *Sidney Papers, CSP Ireland IV*, 150 G. B. Harrison, *The Life and Death of Robert Devereux, Earl of Essex* (London: Cassell, 1937), pp. 227–50.
2. J. E. Neale, *Queen Elizabeth I* (London: Jonathan Cape, 1934), pp. 106–7.
3. Don Carlos, heir to the Spanish throne, was a sadist whose cruelty appalled even his own father. Yet as with so many figures from the

sixteenth century, his life was transformed by Romantic writers and composers such as Schiller and Verdi. For them, the tragedy of Don Carlos is not that of a mentally ill young man who was finally murdered by his own father's command, but that of a young prince whose dream of happiness is destroyed forever when his tyrannical father marries the woman destined to be his son's bride. The monstrous father, symbol of the tyrants against whom a whole generation of young nationalists were fighting in the nineteenth century has supplanted the real version of the story, in which the son was the monster and the father a brooding, depressive ruler who felt compelled to dispose of his inadequate heir.

4. Conyers Read, *Mr Secretary Cecil and Queen Elizabeth* (London: Jonathan Cape, 1955), p. 315.
5. Quoted in Johnson, *Elizabeth I: A Study in Power and Intellect* (London: Weidenfeld & Nicolson, 1974), p. 162.
6. Letter from Elizabeth to Mary Stuart, 24 February 1567, repr. in G. B. Harrison, *The Letters of Queen Elizabeth* (London: Cassell, 1935), p. 49.
7. Elizabeth to Mary Stuart, 23 June 1567, repr. ibid., pp. 50–1.
8. Elizabeth to Mary Stuart, repr. ibid., pp. 103–4.
9. Quoted in Johnson, *Elizabeth*, p. 277.
10. Elizabeth to the deputation of Parliament urging her to execute Mary, quoted in Frederick Chamberlin, *The Sayings of Queen Elizabeth* (London: Bodley Head, 1923), pp. 240–3.
11. Elizabeth to Mary Stuart, October 1586, quoted in Harrison, *Letters*, p. 181.
12. *André Heurault, Sieur de Maisse*, ed. G. B. Harrison and R. A. Jones (London: Nonesuch, 1931).
13. Elizabeth to Francis Bacon, quoted in Chamberlin, *Sayings*, p. 277.
14. Elizabeth to Robert Devereux Earl of Essex, repr. in Harrison, *Letters*, pp. 274–6.
15. Quoted in Johnson, *Elizabeth*, pp. 430–1.
16. *The Diary of John Manningham* (London: Camden Society, 1868), entry for 23 March 1603.

Conclusion

> Much suspected of me,
> Nothing proved can be . . .

Elizabeth I was a powerful woman who aroused strong feelings in those who came into contact with her, and she has continued to arouse strong feelings among her many biographers, both writers of fiction and historians. The many different versions of her life, the varied assessments of her capabilities and the attempts to analyse her psychology show the extent of the fascination she has continued to exert even from the grave. It is not possible to write about such a woman without taking up a position; even those who claim to have worked objectively (if such a thing is possible) show only too plainly where they stand. In these different versions we encounter Elizabeth the despot, Elizabeth the lover, Elizabeth the inadequate monarch, Elizabeth the incomplete woman and many others. On the whole, and with of course a few notable exceptions, historians writing about her have been male while most novelists have been female and this has also contributed to the process of constructing a written portrait of Elizabeth, just as the political position of the writer and his or her religious standpoint have also been significant.

There is a strain running through the work of even the most eminent historians that reveals an uneasiness about Elizabeth's sex. This is manifested most obviously in the way in which Elizabeth's tactics of vacillation and her constant changes of mind have been described pejoratively as quintessentially 'feminine'. Based on the idea firstly that women are less decisive than men and secondly that decisiveness is an important quality for a person in a position of command, Elizabeth's indecisiveness has been viewed as typical of her sex. This, it seems to me, is both over-simplistic and patronising. In the early years of her life, Elizabeth learned that to hold an inflexible position could mean death; at her father's court men died on the block for maintaining fixed positions, and Catherine of Aragon and her daughter Mary, who refused to compromise, lived out their lives in embitterment as a result. Moved from preferment at court to penury in the country apparently at whim, watching in the wings as first her Protestant younger brother swung religious policy in one direction and then her Catholic elder sister swung it in the other, Elizabeth learned that flexibility could mean survival. She saw that the court was perpetually full of spies and observers, watching her every move, recording her every phrase and inventing things she did not say at all. In such an environment, the only way to thrive must have seemed to be to refuse to be pinned down. If she gave no direct answers, made so specific statements, kept silent on controversial issues and generalised when asked hard questions, she could keep the good will of different factions and keep her head into the bargain. This tactic worked so well in her youth that it must have become second nature. As monarch, she continued to use it, surer now in the strength of her position and therefore deliberately choosing to keep even those closest to her in a state of permanent insecurity. Unlike Mary Tudor or Mary Stuart, who laid out the contents of their hearts on the table, Elizabeth locked hers in a closet and furthermore, she also hid the key. Rather than interpreting this character trait as quintessentially feminine, it is more useful to see it for what it was — a behavioural pattern learned in childhood and carried to extremes once she was out of immediate danger. It is the clue to Elizabeth's survival.

Further evidence that this was a learned pattern of behaviour can be found in the traces left by Elizabeth of her own voice. Wherever possible in this book I have let Elizabeth speak for herself; the voice that comes across through her poems, letters, prayers and speeches does not waver; when committing herself to paper, the vacillation disappears. Writing to Mary Stuart after Darnley's murder, upbraiding the bishops who refused to acknowledge her religious reforms, writing in a fury to Robert Dudley who had disobeyed her instructions in the Netherlands, she set aside game-playing and put her feelings on to the stage. The vitality of her letters still amazes; they are full of excitement, energy, emotion and humour. As a writer of fiction in a later age she might have resembled George Eliot, with a sense of humanity and a refined wit.

A dominant motif in her other writing is the wheel of fortune, that could cast an individual down as swiftly as it could raise another up. In the prayers, the turning of fortune's wheel is treated as a sign of God's power, but in her poetry and her translations she returns repeatedly to this theme, showing how deeply it engaged her thoughts. Primarily a medieval motif, it was to disappear as the work ethic of the Reformation, countered by the disciplined inflexibility of the Counter-Reformation, spreading across Europe. This shows yet another way the extent to which Elizabeth was a child of the age of Humanism, an age that was coming to an end in her own lifetime.

The age of Elizabeth is remembered as one of great movement. During her reign the religious compromise that generated the Church of England was established, and certainly she played a large part in this herself, bringing her own brand of tolerance and slightly old-fashioned conservatism into the debate. During her reign also England finally freed itself from the threat of invasion from Spain and the rebellion in Ireland was quelled. These achievements enhanced English prestige at home and abroad, but both cost Elizabeth a good deal of personal anguish. Less successful were the economic shifts — the enclosure of common lands, the rise in the number of property speculators and land-hungry gentry, the spread of monopolies, the corruption among the new nobility, the establishment of the slave trade and the beginnings of colonial profiteering and exploitation. Recalling the greatness of the Elizabethan years, it is often possible to side-step these negative developments, and some blame must be apportioned to Elizabeth herself, who often turned a blind eye to corrupt practices, particularly when her special favourites were involved.

The corruption in the army and the amount of money wasted in overseas campaigns has often been noted. It might with some justice be argued that Elizabeth's sex was a contributing factor to these shortcomings. Since she had never experienced military life of any kind (and never left England from the day of her birth until the day she died) she had no opportunity to experience at first hand mismanagement in the army and navy. She was informed about it, of course — she even tried to hold inquiries into particularly bad cases of abuse — but ultimately she was powerless to resist the might of her generals. During the Netherlands campaign in 1586–7 she tried to discover exactly what was happening to the money which disappeared as soon as it was allocated. Soldiers were unpaid and starving, and the money sent for their wages vanished before it could be spent. When a crowd of ex-soldiers appeared at the court gates starving and arguing that they should not be classified as vagabonds, Elizabeth tried to hold an inquiry into the causes of their distress. Not only were the captains responsible for the ongoing fraud never brought to justice, but they were frequently granted even greater privileges. At one point Leicester knighted fourteen captains in a single day, and later, during the Irish campaign, Essex ennobled many of his own corrupt henchmen. The closed world of the army where fortunes could be made by those in command was beyond Elizabeth's powers, try as she might, and this was principally due to her being a woman.

The abuse of power by military commanders and their deliberate refusal to allow the Queen to intervene on behalf of the common soldiers exposes the ambiguity towards Elizabeth that was so often carefully concealed. From the beginning of her reign, she had been hailed as an idealised figure, a Virgin ruler embodying all the virtues, the moon goddess in her earthly form. During her reign, tributes to her greatness became ever more grandiose, and after her death a process of beatification began, with Elizabeth hailed as the harbinger of a new Protestant dawn, a new golden age. Yet at the same time, the Queen was being blatantly used and abused, carefully prevented from knowing certain facts by her advisers and milked for financial rewards and social advancement by the courtiers who flocked around her. In her speeches she constantly stresses the gap between her body (female) and her mind or spirit, which she maintained was that of a king (male). That she did this so often suggests that it was probably more than a straightforward rhetorical device to win sympathy from her listeners, but rose from a deliberate and sincere intention to convey that she was by no means the weak creature she was held to be, but one well able to hold her own in a male-dominated world.

A letter of December 1561 from Cecil, her trusted adviser, to Throckmorton, written during the Scottish war crisis, reveals something of the complex interaction between himself and Elizabeth:

I have carried in my head with care means how her Majesty

should, from time to time, conduct her affairs. But I see so
small proof of my travails, by reason her Majesty alloweth not
of them, that I have left all to the wide world. I do only keep on
a course for show, but inwardly I meddle not, leaving things to
run in a course as the clock is left when the barrel is wound
up. . . .[1]

Conyers Read's detailed study of the relationship between Elizabeth and Cecil provides fascinating documentation, but leaves
many questions unanswered. Cecil saw it as integral to his role to
shape Elizabeth's mind and policy; he was attached to the
Protestant cause and held strong feelings on certain key issues,
such as the need for the Queen to marry. Often he patronised her,
sometimes he deliberately kept her in ignorance of crucial facts.
Nevertheless, in her dealings with him, Elizabeth matched his
careful determination with her own special skills. Her refusal to
commit herself infuriated Cecil frequently, and made it difficult
for him to ensure that his plans were put into effect. Sifting
through the evidence, it seems to be apparent that Cecil believed
in the fundamental superiority of the male sex (and if Cecil did,
then so also did the rest of the court and council) and Elizabeth
had to use different strategies to combat this prejudice. Many
have chosen to see Elizabeth's virginity as a sign of some sexual
or psychological inadequacy, but it makes more sense to see it as
a political statement. By remaining a virgin Elizabeth could
avoid the immediate risk of being seen to be the inferior partner
in the marriage relationship, and she could maintain a position of
special privilege as a woman that not even her status as Queen
could bestow upon her.

Virginity in the medieval world was accorded a high status.
Only with the advent of the Reformation did marriage, as a
symbol of the active life, come to be seen as superior to the inner,
contemplative ideal of virginity. Holding as she did to many of
the old values, it is not surprising that Elizabeth also perceived
the latter as being a higher state than that of matrimony. Moreover, her virginity in a world in which power-politics and
marriage were inextricably connected, enabled her to occupy a
special position: she could refuse marriage and subjugation and
still keep all her prestige. That she had what could be described
as a marital relationship with Robert Dudley (and even the

relationship with Cecil, though asexual, had its domestic dimension) is irrelevant before the stark fact of her sustained image of the Virgin Queen. Elizabeth's virginity was her statement of what we might term feminist attitude; in the world of the court where sexual licence prevailed, it set her apart, and though some decried her hypocrisy in maintaining the image of a vestal virgin while having Dudley moved to a bedroom adjoining her own, the public statement prevailed. It was her trump card; having played it she had no alternative but to accept the consequences of her game.

Although Elizabeth's virginity makes sense in terms of the age in which she lived, it has been harder for later commentators, influenced by the idea that a woman is only fulfilled by having a husband and children, to accept her choice. The bleak picture of Elizabeth as a lonely, eccentric old woman in a court full of pushy, sensual young men and women is a striking one. In recent years this image of her old age has often been highlighted; in the series of plays on her life for BBC Television, Glenda Jackson portrayed the ageing Elizabeth as a sharp-tongued harridan, heavily painted and grotesquely ugly. Dario Fo's play *Elizabeth: Almost By Chance a Woman*, first performed in 1984, gives us the image of a hideous old woman (played by Gillian Hanna) completely bald beneath her lurid red wig, a symbol of the corruption of an age that marked the beginnings of imperialist expansion.

These images of grotesquerie and decay are twentieth-century additions to an existing wealth of iconographic motifs of Elizabeth. During her lifetime there was a proliferation of portraits, miniatures and representations of Elizabeth of all kinds, and as Sir Roy Strong has shown, she seems to have been presented in an increasingly idealised manner, with her skirts becoming larger and more ornate, her ruffs wider and higher, her hair more bejewelled and her hands more white and thin. Discussing the Ditchley portrait of 1592 (plate 4) and contrasting it with the portrait of the young Elizabeth of *c*.1545 (plate 1) he comments:

The cheeks once filled with the bloom of youth have become sunken and rouged; the eyes have the penetration of one for whom life has been an unceasing battle of wits; the lips are thin and mean; the face wrinkled, almost haggard in appearance; in short the young girl has become the great Queen whose genius has guided victoriously the destinies of a people for over thirty years. The painter of the first saw her as a slip of a girl, the painter of the second as a ruler of legendary fame, a visionary figure towering above her realm of England, an image of almost cosmic power. In a span of forty years an individual has been transposed into a symbol. To place side by side these two portraits is to pose visually the problems of the portraits of Queen Elizabeth I.[2]

Writing this personal account of Elizabeth, I find myself drawn to certain images of her rather than to others. Like all the other biographers, novelists and historians, I have my own prejudices that condition the way in which I see my material. Her Coronation Portrait (plate 2) is an image that seems to me to say a great deal. It is highly stylised, a full frontal view of the young Queen holding her orb and sceptre and wearing the heavy gold robes of state, ornamented with ermine. Her red hair, certainly not a wig at this stage in her life, is spread out across her shoulders and the crown sits rather primly on her head. What appeals about this portrait is the clear gaze of the woman in the picture; she stares out straight into the eyes of the observer, and the heavy robes seem almost to float rather than weigh her down. It is an optimistic portrait, a suggestive image of a woman with a mind of her own about to embark on a great task.

The second image that comes to mind when I think of Elizabeth is the strong stone face on her tomb in Westminster Abbey (plate 5). All the details that have become so familiar from the stylised portraits are missing — her lips are full, rather than thin, her jowls are heavy, her face is long and her chin is inclined to fat. The sharp-featured weasel-like qualities so often associated with early portraits of Elizabeth have vanished in old age; the carefully arranged ringlets may be a wig, or they may be the thinning grey hair she died with. The eyes are quite blank. In contrast to the Coronation portrait, everything in this sculpture, which was probably carved from a death-mask, gives the impression of weightiness and solidity. The Elizabeth of the tomb is a monolithic figure, a rather coarse-featured woman with a large nose and a set mouth. Between the two images, between the cool straight gaze and the blank, eyeless stare, is the complex, ambiguous life story of this multi-faceted woman.

Between these two images, one of beginning and the other of stony end, I came across a third, one that has nothing to do with Renaissance reality but which speaks to the late twentieth-century mind: the German actress Sonya Kehler playing Elizabeth in breeches, a reminder of the world in which Elizabeth moved and a symbol of activity and energy. The major female roles that have become so familiar to us, from Juliet to Lady Macbeth, from Ophelia to Rosalind, were all played by males on the Elizabethan stage. Woman could be represented symbolically, portrayed by a man in female clothing, but woman as herself could not appear. This contradiction, which developed during the years of rule by a woman monarch, is further evidence of the great gap between our perceptions of sexuality and gender roles today and those prevalent in the Renaissance. By presenting us with an image of Elizabeth, dressed as Viola might have appeared (that same character who would have been played by a male), Kehler reminds us of the distance between the two worlds. Here, in our own time, we construct an Elizabeth according to signs and conventions of today, even though we may try to comprehend some of the differences between this age and Elizabeth's. But Rosalind and Viola have been played by women now for so long, that the values they embody have been totally feminised. From being a joke, as men dressed up as women disguised themselves as men within their roles, the breeches part has become a way of emphasising femaleness, and at the same time hinting at the other world of independent, male activity. Elizabeth on a stage in farthingale and ruff is a comfortably familiar image from the past, a reconstruction of what we think might once have been. But Elizabeth dressed in doublet and hose is a reminder instead of the ambiguities in her life and in our image of her. We may romanticise her in different ways and fantasise about her life, but the anomaly of what she was still has to be confronted. In an age when women were losing ground, when the enlightened vision of the Humanist age was disappearing in the smoke of religious intolerance and institutions began to acquire more power than the individuals caught up in them, Elizabeth as woman ruler was an anomaly and a mystery, embodying both the male and the female, yet very far from being androgynous. In her last great speech in 1601, she again makes statements about her sex and her strength, arguing that the qualities she has brought as ruler, the 'zeal to my country, care to my subjects', her bravery and willingness to sacrifice herself are not the exclusive properties of men: 'Should I ascribe anything to myself as to my sexly weakness, I were not worthy to live then and of all most unworthy of the mercies I have had from God, who hath ever yet given me a heart which never yet feared foreign or home enemies.'[3]

This statement, made at the end of her life, stands as a testament to her own sex. Far from being an inadequate woman or a quasi-man, Elizabeth should be seen as a woman who struggled against anti-feminist prejudice and who has remained a symbol of active female assertiveness for future generations.

Notes

1. Letter from Cecil to Throckmorton, 22 December 1561, quoted in Conyers Read, *Mr Secretary Cecil and Queen Elizabeth* (London: Jonathan Cape, 1955), p. 233.
2. Roy Strong, *The Portraits of Queen Elizabeth I* (Oxford: Clarendon Press, 1963, updated 1987), p. 3.
3. Quoted in Frederick Chamberlin, *The Sayings of Queen Elizabeth* (London: Bodley Head, 1923), p. 51.

Chronology

1533   Elizabeth born on Sunday, 3 September at Greenwich to King Henry VIII and Anne Boleyn.

1536   Anne Boleyn executed for treason. Henry marries Jane Seymour. Catherine Champernowne (Kat Ashley) enters Elizabeth's service.

1537   Edward, Elizabeth's brother, born to Henry VIII and Jane Seymour. Elizabeth declared a bastard. Jane Seymour dies.

1539   Henry marries Anne of Cleves, from whom he separates almost immediately.

1540   Henry marries Catherine Howard, cousin of Anne Boleyn.

1542   Catherine Howard executed.

1543   Henry marries his sixth wife, Catherine Parr, for whom Elizabeth translates *The Glasse of the Sinfull Soule* in 1544.

1547   Henry VIII dies. Elizabeth takes up residence with Catherine Parr in Chelsea.

1548   Elizabeth leaves Catherine Parr's household in slightly dubious circumstances. Rumours circulate about her affair with Thomas Seymour. Catherine dies in childbirth in September.

1549   Thomas Seymour tried for treason and executed. Elizabeth and her household closely questioned by Sir Robert Tyrwhit.

1551   Elizabeth is welcomed back into London from self-imposed retreat at Hatfield and received at court.

1553   Edward VI dies. Mary, Elizabeth's elder sister

becomes Queen after the Protestant coup led by Northumberland fails to have her cousin, Lady Jane Grey, accepted as rightful Queen.

1554	Elizabeth imprisoned in the Tower of London suspected of plotting against Mary. She is released two months later and sent to Woodstock in Oxfordshire, guarded by Sir Henry Bedingfield. In July Mary marries Philip of Spain.
1555–8	Elizabeth in and out of favour with Mary. Mary's persecution of Protestant heretics increases.
1558	Mary dies on 17 November. Elizabeth becomes Queen.
1560	Amy Robsart, wife of Elizabeth's favourite Robert Dudley, dies. Rumours of her murder effectively destroy any hopes of Elizabeth marrying Dudley.
1561	Mary Queen of Scots returns to Scotland from France.
1562	Elizabeth contracts smallpox.
1565	Mary marries Lord Darnley, strengthening her claim to Elizabeth's crown.
1567	Darnley murdered. Mary marries Lord Bothwell, is captured and imprisoned in Edinburgh.
1568	Mary escapes, flees to England and is held in confinement by Elizabeth.
1569–70	The Northern Rising.
1570–1	The Ridolfi Plot.
1570	The Papal Bull, *Regnans in Excelsis* excommunicates Elizabeth and frees Catholics of allegiance to her sovereignty.
1572	St Bartholomew's Day Massacre in Paris, 24 August.
1575–6	Crisis in the Low Countries.

1578	Negotiations for marriage between Elizabeth and the Duke of Alençon begin (marriage plans are not finally abandoned until 1581).
1579	John Stubbs and William Page have their right hands cut off for publishing a pamphlet opposing Elizabeth's marriage to Alençon.
1585	Elizabeth sends English troops into the Low Countries.
1586	The Babington Plot.
1587	Execution of Mary Queen of Scots for conspiracy against Elizabeth.
1588	The defeat of the Spanish Armada. Robert Dudley, now Earl of Leicester, dies. Elizabeth creates his stepson, the Earl of Essex, her Master of the Horse.
1589	Elizabeth loses old and trusted friends — death of Blanche Parry, waiting woman since 1545; death of Sir Christopher Hatton. Henri III of France is assassinated. Elizabeth becomes embroiled in military intervention in France to assist Huguenot successor.
1595	Hugh O'Neill, Earl of Tyrone, challenges English rule of Ireland.
1598	Death of William Cecil, Lord Burghley. Elizabeth sends a major expedition to suppress the Irish Rising.
1599	Essex given command of the Irish expeditionary force. He fails to crush the rebellion, returns to London against Elizabeth's orders.
1600	Essex leads an unsuccessful rebellion against Elizabeth.
1601	Essex executed for treason. Lord Mountjoy finally quells the Irish rebels. Tyrone surrenders.
1603	Elizabeth's close friend and cousin, the Countess of Nottingham, dies in February. Elizabeth retreats

into melancholia.

24 March, Elizabeth dies.

28 April, Elizabeth's state funeral. She is buried in Westminster Abbey.

James VI of Scotland, son of Mary Queen of Scots, succeeds as James I of England.

Select Bibliography

Good bibliographies are included in both Erikson and Paul Johnson; for original sources or documents readers are recommended to consult the appropriate *Calendar of State Papers* (all published in London by Longman), in particular the following: [CSP] *Domestic Series, of the Reigns of Edward VI, Mary, Elizabeth and James I*, 12 vols., ed. Robert Lemon and Mary A. E. Green (1856–72); [CSP] *Foreign Series, of the Reign of Edward VI, 1547–1553*, ed. William B. Turnbull (1861); [CSP] *Foreign Series, of the Reign of Mary, 1553–1558*, ed. William B. Turnbull (1861); [CSP] *Foreign Series, of the Reign of Elizabeth*, 23 vols., ed. William B. Turnbull et al. (1863–1950).

Black, J. B., *The Reign of Elizabeth 1558–1603* (Oxford: The Clarendon Press, 1936)

Bradner, Leicester, *The Poems of Queen Elizabeth I* (Providence, Rhode Island: Brown University Press, 1964)

Buxton, John, *Elizabethan Taste* (Brighton: Harvester, 1983)

Camden, William, *The History of the Most Renowned and Victorious Princess Elizabeth, Late Queen of England*, 4th edn (London: R. Bentley, 1688; repr. New York: AMS Press, 1970)

Chamberlin, F., *The Sayings of Queen Elizabeth* (London: John Lane, Bodley Head, 1923)

Erikson, Carrolly, *The First Elizabeth* (London: Macmillan, 1983)

Fo, Dario, trans. Gillian Hanna, *Elizabeth: Almost by chance a woman* (London: Methuen, 1987)

Greaves, Richard L. (ed.), *Elizabeth I, Queen of England* (Lexington, Mass.: D.C. Heath, 1974)

Gurr, Andrew, *The Shakespearean Stage, 1574–1642* (Cambridge: Cambridge University Press, 1970)

Haigh, Christopher (ed.), *The Reign of Elizabeth I* (London: Macmillan, 1984)

Harrison, G. B. (ed.), *The Letters of Queen Elizabeth* (London: Cassell, 1935)

Hayward, John, *Annals of the First Four Years of the Reign of Queen*

Elizabeth, ed. John Bruce, Camden Society, Old Series, VII (London: J. B. Nichols, 1840)

Irwin, Margaret, Young Bess; *Elizabeth and the Prince of Spain*; and Elizabeth, Captive Princess (London: Chatto & Windus, 1956)

Jenkins, Elizabeth, *Elizabeth the Great* (London: Odhams, 1958)

Johnson, Paul, *Elizabeth I: A Study in Power and Intellect* (London: Weidenfeld & Nicolson, 1974)

Klarwill, Victor von (ed.), *Queen Elizabeth and Some Foreigners* (New York: Brentano, 1928)

MacCaffrey, Wallace, *The Shaping of the Elizabethan Regime* (London: Jonathan Cape, 1969)

Maclean, Ian, *The Renaissance Notion of Woman* (Cambridge: Cambridge University Press, 1970).

Meyer, Arnold Oskar, *England and the Catholic Church Under Queen Elizabeth*, trans. Rev. J. R. McKee (London: Routledge and Kegan Paul, 1967)

Mumby, Frank O., *The Girlhood of Queen Elizabeth: A Narrative in Contemporary Letters* (London: Constable, 1909)

Neale, John E., *Queen Elizabeth I* (London: Jonathan Cape, 1934, repr. Harmondsworth: Penguin, 1960)

——, *Elizabeth I and Her Parliaments*, vol. I: *1559–1581*, vol. II: *1584–1601* (London: Jonathan Cape, 1949–57)

Nichols, John, *The Progresses and Public Processions of Queen Elizabeth*, new edn, 3 vols. (London: John Nichols and Son, 1823, repr. New York: AMS Press, 1969)

Plaidy, Jean, *Queen of this Realm* (London: Robert Hale, 1984)

Read, Conyers, *Mr Secretary Walsingham and the Policy of Queen Elizabeth*, 3 vols. (Oxford: Oxford University Press, 1925

——, *Mr Secretary Cecil and Queen Elizabeth* (London: Jonathan Cape, 1955)

——, *Lord Burghley and Queen Elizabeth* (London: Jonathan Cape, 1960)

Rowse, A. L., *The Elizabethan Renaissance: The Cultural Achievement* (London: Macmillan, 1972)

Strickland, Agnes, *Lives of the Queens of England*, 8 vols. (London: Henry Colburn, 1851)

Strong, Roy, *Portraits of Queen Elizabeth I* (Oxford: The Clarendon Press, 1963, revised edn, 1987)

——, and Julia Trevelyan, *Elizabeth R.* (London: Secker & Warburg, 1971)

Wernham, R. B., *The Making of Elizabethan Foreign Policy, 1558–1603* (Berkeley and Los Angeles: University of California Press, 1980)

Williams, Neville, *The Life and Times of Elizabeth I* (London: Weidenfeld and Nicolson, 1972)

Wright, Thomas (ed.), *Queen Elizabeth and Her Times*, 2 vols. (London: Henry Colburn, 1838)

Yates, Frances A., *Astraea: The Imperial Theme in the Sixteenth Century* (London: Routledge & Kegan Paul, 1975)

Index